Riba Exposed: How Islam Challenges the Global Interest System

MAA

Published by MAA, 2025.

RIBA EXPOSED: HOW ISLAM CHALLENGES THE GLOBAL INTEREST SYSTEM

First edition. June 11, 2025.

ISBN: 979-8231349180

Written by MAA.

Chapter 1: The Genesis of Trade and Debt in Ancient Societies

Long before the written word, human beings traded. In the open air of ancient river valleys and along dusty footpaths winding through early settlements, trade was an instinctive form of survival. The first economies were not built on coins or contracts but on need, memory, and trust. A fisherman gave a portion of his catch to a potter in exchange for a vessel. A herder offered goatskin in return for barley. These were transactions born of immediacy and simplicity, built on barter—direct exchange without a common medium.

As populations grew and specialization intensified, barter systems struggled to keep pace. The problem of *coincidence of wants*—needing what the other has at the same time—posed increasing friction. To resolve this, early societies began to use standardized goods as a means of indirect exchange. Grain, salt, cattle, and even cowry shells became early proto-currencies. Yet even these could not eliminate the uncertainty and complexity of trade over time and distance.

In Sumer, nestled between the Tigris and Euphrates rivers around 3000 BCE, humanity took a significant step: it recorded its economic agreements. Clay tablets inscribed with cuneiform script tracked loans of barley and silver. These were not mere notes—they were enforceable contracts. The birth of accounting in Sumer was as much about managing debt as it was about managing trade. Interest was not an invention of modern bankers; it was a known quantity. A Sumerian loan contract might stipulate a return of one and a third for every measure lent. The idea of capital growing over time had entered the human imagination.

In Babylon, debt instruments were formalized further under Hammurabi's Code around 1750 BCE. The code set maximum interest rates: 20% on silver loans, 33⅓% on grain. Penalties were harsh. A defaulting debtor could face slavery, and his family could be sold into servitude. Yet the law also extended some protections—limiting interest rates and banning compound interest in some cases. Babylonian society, with its temples and palaces, functioned on a framework that mixed religious morality with commercial pragmatism. Lending at interest was not only permitted but institutionalized.

Ancient Egypt, too, had its mechanisms for trade and debt, though with less formality than Mesopotamia. Farmers borrowed seed grain from temple stores to plant crops, repaying with the harvest plus a surplus. Priests, acting as custodians of temple wealth, became proto-bankers. The Nile's cycles dictated the pace of repayment, and the concept of delayed return embedded itself into agricultural life.

The story was similar in ancient India. Vedic texts as early as 1500 BCE mention moneylenders (*kusidin*) and interest-bearing loans. The Sanskrit term *usury—kusida*—was known to both the lawgivers and the moralists. While not outright forbidden, interest was looked upon with ambivalence. The *Dharmashastra* texts imposed restrictions, warning of spiritual impurity associated with excess interest, yet offering legal structure for its regulation.

In ancient China, debt and interest also played roles in shaping social hierarchies. The Zhou Dynasty (circa 1046–256 BCE) codified lending laws, including usury limits. Confucian philosophers frowned upon the exploitation of the poor through high interest but accepted modest gains as necessary for social order. The state sometimes intervened, especially during famines, to cancel debts and relieve pressure on the peasantry.

Greek civilization, admired for its philosophy and politics, operated an economy heavily reliant on interest-bearing loans. In classical Athens, commercial lenders—*trapezitai*—offered loans at varying rates, sometimes 12% or more, particularly for maritime trade ventures. These were high-risk, high-reward endeavors. Loans funded ships carrying olive oil, wine, and grain across the Mediterranean.

Interest, in this context, was the price of uncertainty, a hedge against shipwreck and piracy. Yet even here, the moral critique existed. Plato and Aristotle expressed deep discomfort with the notion of money "breeding money." Aristotle in particular criticized usury as unnatural: money, he argued, should be a medium, not an end. To charge interest was to violate the organic nature of exchange.

Rome, the inheritor of Greek culture, adopted and expanded financial practices. Early Roman law permitted interest, but over time, caps were introduced. The *Lex Genucia* (342 BCE) attempted to ban interest altogether, though the prohibition was short-lived. By the time of the late Republic, lending had become a robust and often ruthless enterprise. Wealthy Roman senators lent money to provinces and individuals at punitive rates, using economic leverage as a tool of both political control and personal enrichment. The practice contributed to cycles of rural indebtedness, leading to land concentration and social upheaval.

It was in this crucible of ancient economies that the moral dimension of lending began to take shape. Civilizations wrestled with questions that remain relevant today: How should wealth circulate? Is profit from time legitimate? When does commerce become exploitation? These were not abstract queries—they were urgent, lived realities for the debtor under the thumb of a lender, the tenant forced off land to pay a silver debt, or the merchant who faced ruin over a missed voyage.

In these early societies, debt was not merely an economic relationship. It became a social bond, often laden with spiritual and ethical implications. Temples were central to both trade and finance, and in many cultures, the divine watched over contracts. Debts were forgiven during jubilees, interest was capped by religious decrees, and lenders were warned of divine displeasure for exploiting the vulnerable.

The ancient world had no single answer to the problem of interest. But it had clearly identified the problem. Debt was powerful, and in the wrong hands, destructive. From Sumerian clay tablets to Roman scrolls, the tension between profit and morality was written into the DNA of human civilization.

Chapter 2: Riba in the Pre-Islamic World — Babylon to Byzantium

In the empires that shaped the ancient world, interest on loans was not merely tolerated; it was deeply embedded within law, commerce, and theology. Yet it never escaped controversy. From Babylon to Byzantium, civilizations codified, debated, and sometimes resisted the charging of interest, setting the stage for later religious critiques that would culminate in Islam's outright prohibition of *riba*.

Babylonian Codification and Normalization

The Babylonian economy, especially under the reign of Hammurabi (circa 18th century BCE), functioned with a sophisticated legal and financial system. Hammurabi's Code—etched into stone—outlined specific interest rates: 20% annually for silver loans and 33⅓% for grain. Loans were commonly issued in silver, a stable medium of exchange, while grain, being perishable and dependent on seasonal yields, carried greater risk and thus a higher return.

These interest rates weren't hidden; they were state-sanctioned and culturally accepted. Temples played an instrumental role as both banks and landowners, often issuing loans backed by temple assets. The economy ran on credit, but it was also volatile. Widespread indebtedness among farmers during years of poor harvests led to severe consequences, including debt slavery, confiscation of land, and permanent loss of livelihood.

Kings periodically intervened through royal edicts known as *debt remissions*. These were mass cancellations of debts to prevent social collapse. While not acts of moral resistance to interest itself, these remissions reflect the recognition of its destabilizing impact when left unchecked.

Hebrew Law and the Seeds of Moral Restraint

Ancient Israelite society, in contrast, took a more ambivalent approach. The Torah contains explicit prohibitions against charging interest to fellow Israelites. In Exodus 22:25, the command is unambiguous: *"If you lend money to any of My people who are poor among you, do not be like a moneylender; charge him no interest."* Leviticus and Deuteronomy reinforce this directive, framing interest as a form of oppression, particularly when levied against the poor.

However, the restriction was not universal. Deuteronomy 23:20 permits interest on loans to foreigners, suggesting a distinction between internal community ethics and external commercial dealings. This ethical bifurcation allowed for interest-based transactions in broader trade networks while maintaining a degree of communal protection. Rabbinic interpretations in later centuries continued this tension, gradually reintroducing interest through legal mechanisms like *heter iska*, a workaround that converted loans into profit-sharing ventures in form, if not in spirit.

Greek Rationalism and Economic Pragmatism

The Greek world introduced a philosophical layer to the question of interest. Greek city-states, particularly Athens, were deeply commercial. Maritime trade required large upfront capital outlays and significant risk, especially in unpredictable seas. Lenders to shipowners often demanded high interest—sometimes exceeding 30%—to offset the chance of total loss.

Despite this financial realism, prominent philosophers rejected the moral basis of interest. Plato considered lending at interest unethical, as it monetized social relations and prioritized greed. Aristotle was more direct: he labeled interest as "money breeding money," something unnatural because money, in his view, was sterile and should only serve as a medium of exchange. He argued that wealth should be acquired through productive means—not through the mere passage of time.

Yet the practical Greek economy contradicted these ideals. Wealthy citizens lent money for land purchases, housing, and commercial ventures. Lenders had broad powers in case of default, including seizure of property or even enslavement. Thus, while the philosophers condemned interest, the city-states built their economies partly upon it.

Roman Institutionalization of Interest

Rome inherited the economic structures of the Greeks but advanced them through legal rigor and administrative consistency. Early Roman law, under the Twelve Tables (circa 5th century BCE), permitted interest but capped it at *uncia centesima*—roughly 1% per month, or 12% annually. Over time, the caps shifted in response to social pressure and political instability. The Lex Genucia of 342 BCE famously attempted to ban interest altogether, but enforcement proved elusive. Loans persisted, interest continued, and lenders adapted.

As the Roman Republic gave way to the Empire, debt became a political weapon. The senatorial class often doubled as creditors, lending to provinces at high interest and then using unpaid debts as a pretext for political intervention or even annexation. Peasants in Italy and provincial farmers alike suffered under cycles of debt that led to land loss and migration to urban centers.

To ease unrest, some emperors enacted debt relief. Julius Caesar canceled a portion of debts after the civil war; Nero later imposed interest rate limits and penalized exploitative lenders. Yet these reforms never touched the core of the issue. Rome needed credit to expand and maintain its imperial system. Temples, guilds, and later Christian institutions took part in the financial structure, often becoming both religious centers and fiscal hubs.

Zoroastrian Ambiguity in Persia

In ancient Persia, the Zoroastrian worldview emphasized cosmic duality: truth versus falsehood, justice versus oppression. While the sacred texts of Zoroastrianism do not explicitly address interest, the broader ethical framework disapproved of economic exploitation. Lending was permitted, but profiteering at the expense of others' hardship was discouraged. Sassanian legal records show regulated loan practices and occasional interest limits.

Religious scholars debated whether charging interest was compatible with *asha*—the principle of truth and order central to Zoroastrian ethics. Persian rulers, needing to finance military campaigns and infrastructure, allowed lending practices that carried interest, but always under the eye of imperial regulation.

Byzantine Christianity and Doctrinal Tension

In the Byzantine Empire, shaped by Roman governance and Christian doctrine, attitudes toward interest took a decisive turn. Early Church Fathers such as St. Basil, St. Ambrose, and St. Augustine condemned usury outright. They considered it un-Christian to profit from another's need, citing Christ's example and the parables against greed. The First Council of Nicaea in 325 CE forbade clergy from charging interest, a rule later extended to all lay Christians.

Byzantine emperors issued periodic bans on usury. The most famous was Justinian I's codification in the 6th century, which both capped interest rates and criminalized excessive lending. Yet the complexity of Byzantine commerce—especially in urban Constantinople—meant that lending continued in various forms. Merchants used commercial partnerships and equity contracts to circumvent strict interpretations. The prohibition of interest increasingly became a moral posture rather than a universally applied policy.

Byzantine canon law struggled to maintain its opposition to interest as the empire grew more dependent on long-distance trade and capital mobility. Eventually, Byzantine society developed a dual standard: while interest was condemned theologically, it was permitted under strict legal supervision, reflecting a broader pattern of ethical compromise for political and economic survival.

Chapter 3: Arabia Before Islam — Social Structures and Economic Exploitation

In the centuries leading up to the advent of Islam, the Arabian Peninsula was a patchwork of tribal alliances, nomadic traditions, and emerging urban centers. Makkah, Yathrib, Ta'if, and other towns acted as nodes of commerce and culture in an otherwise harsh and fragmented desert landscape. While Arabia lacked the imperial bureaucracy of Rome or Persia, it fostered an economy that combined pastoralism, trade caravans, small-scale agriculture, and localized forms of finance.

Makkah in particular stood out—not only for its religious significance due to the Kaaba but also as a commercial hub. The Quraysh tribe, who controlled Makkah, had established seasonal trade routes stretching north toward Byzantine Syria and south toward Yemen. These routes passed through tribal territories that the Quraysh skillfully negotiated with payments, alliances, and sometimes intimidation. Their caravans transported goods such as spices, leather, textiles, incense, and precious metals. This mercantile culture produced wealth, but it also embedded financial practices that were exploitative at their core.

Among these was the practice of lending money on interest—*riba*—a system that preyed upon those with limited means. Contracts were oral but binding, enforced through tribal custom and honor. Interest was not just tolerated; it was normalized. A typical debt arrangement involved a creditor lending money or goods with an agreed-upon time for repayment. If the debtor failed to repay on time, the lender would extend the term—at a cost. The new amount owed would include the original principal plus an increased amount, agreed upon either as a lump sum or as a recurring percentage.

This compounding structure could rapidly spiral. A debtor defaulting once could find himself owing double or more in subsequent cycles. Tribes were close-knit, but their economics were unforgiving. Debtors unable to fulfill their obligations could be subjected to humiliation, seizure of assets, or enslavement. In extreme cases, family members—especially sons—could be taken as collateral. Women and children were not spared; their value was often reduced to market worth when debts were being collected.

The tribal society operated on a strict hierarchy. Nobles and chieftains held political and economic power, while clients and freedmen lived under their protection in exchange for loyalty or labor. In this stratified order, wealth served as a means of control. Rich merchants acted as informal banks, extending credit to poorer clans or individuals. These debts often came with conditions that stripped the borrower of land, livestock, or personal freedom if unpaid.

Urbanization in Makkah further cemented these dynamics. As trade increased, more formalized commercial contracts developed. The Quraysh merchants maintained ledgers and conducted business with caravan leaders, farmers, and craftspeople. Trust remained important, but financial pressure eroded community solidarity. Seasonal droughts, poor harvests, or misfortunes in trade caravans could quickly devastate families dependent on credit to survive.

Beyond commercial loans, *riba* also found its way into social obligations. Weddings, funerals, and tribal feuds required expenditures that many could not afford upfront. Wealthier clans loaned money to poorer ones to manage these occasions, charging interest under the guise of assistance. What appeared to be generosity was, in many cases, a calculated method of acquiring long-term leverage.

The Quraysh elite benefited from this system. Their wealth grew not merely from trade, but from the interest collected on loans extended to both individuals and clans. This concentration of wealth allowed them to exert influence over Makkah's social and political order. They constructed homes near the Kaaba, appointed themselves as custodians of sacred sites, and set the rules of arbitration for trade and disputes. Power and money became inseparable.

Poetry from the pre-Islamic era reflects the harshness of these conditions. Arab poets often lamented the degradation of debt, the loss of dignity it caused, and the cruelty of creditors. The poet al-Mutalammis described the borrower as someone whose soul was sold, whose honor dissolved by the weight of obligation. These were not metaphors; they reflected a lived experience where economic bondage could rival physical slavery.

Slavery itself intersected with financial systems. People indebted beyond recovery were sometimes sold or sold themselves into slavery to settle what they owed. Others offered their children in repayment. Slaves were not only war captives or tribal outsiders; many were originally free people destroyed by mounting debt. Lenders had the legal and customary right to claim persons as property, reinforcing a cycle of impoverishment that devastated the most vulnerable.

Religious practices of the time did little to curb this system. Arabian paganism, though rich in ritual, lacked a unified ethical or legal framework to regulate economic behavior. While certain tribes maintained codes of honor, these codes prioritized tribal prestige and revenge over fairness in trade. Pilgrimage seasons brought temporary truces, but they also intensified commercial activity, leading to even greater accumulation of debt for those who came to trade but returned with obligations.

In cities like Yathrib (later Madinah), agriculture played a larger role, particularly among the Jewish tribes who practiced both farming and moneylending. Jewish financial practices in Arabia drew from their own legal tradition, which distinguished between charging interest to fellow Jews and to outsiders. Arab tribes in Madinah sometimes borrowed from Jewish lenders with agreed-upon interest rates, a practice that would later become a source of social friction and political negotiation.

By the sixth century CE, Arabia stood at the crossroads of old and new worlds. The Persian and Byzantine empires loomed on the horizon, their financial systems echoing into Arabia through trade and travel. Yet within the peninsula, economic systems remained unregulated, tribal in character, and prone to abuse. Wealth consolidated into the hands of a few. The poor bore the weight of both seasonal hardship and systemic exploitation. Debt and interest were so deeply woven into society that they were rarely questioned—only endured.

It was into this environment that a radically different economic ethic would soon be revealed. But in pre-Islamic Arabia, *riba* was not just a financial tool. It was a mechanism of control, a structure of inequality, and a silent engine behind much of the social suffering that Islam would later confront head-on.

Chapter 4: The Quranic Revelation — The First Condemnations of Riba

The revelation of the Qur'an unfolded over a span of twenty-three years, in a society that normalized lending practices built on exploitation. Within this environment, the Qur'an's condemnation of *riba* arrived not abruptly but gradually, revealing a layered and deliberate process of moral and legal transformation. It was a rejection not only of unjust transactions but of an entire framework that made inequality systemic and unchallenged.

The earliest verses addressing economic justice did not mention *riba* directly. Instead, they spoke in broad ethical terms—promoting fairness in trade, urging mercy toward the poor, and warning of the moral decay caused by greed. These foundational principles prepared the ground for more specific prohibitions. In Makkahn verses, justice was emphasized as a central divine expectation, and acts of charity were exalted as signs of righteousness. The believer was called not only to pray, but also to protect the orphan, feed the hungry, and avoid hoarding wealth.

It was in the later Madinahn phase of revelation—after the migration of the Prophet Muhammad (pbuh) to Yathrib (Madinah)—that the Qur'an addressed *riba* directly. By then, the Muslim community had developed into a political and economic entity, and the Qur'an began issuing regulations for social and commercial life. The first reference appears in **Surat al-Rum (30:39)**:

> *"Whatever you give as interest to increase your wealth from the property of others will not increase with Allah, but what you give in charity, seeking the pleasure of Allah—those are the ones who will get a manifold increase."*

This verse draws a sharp contrast between two economic behaviors: one rooted in self-interest, the other in selflessness. It introduces the idea that interest-based gains may appear fruitful in worldly terms but are spiritually bankrupt. The contrast is not merely financial—it is moral, drawing a boundary between human calculation and divine valuation.

As the Madinan community matured, the condemnations grew stronger. **Surat al-Nisa (4:161)** notes the wrongdoing of previous communities:

> *"And for their taking of riba while they had been forbidden from it, and their devouring of people's wealth unjustly, We have prepared for the disbelievers among them a painful punishment."*

Here, the reference is retrospective—citing the Israelites who transgressed divine law. The message links *riba* to systemic injustice and moral corruption, placing it in continuity with past religious violations. It also hints at accountability that transcends legal systems: divine judgment based on exploitation.

The strongest and most explicit condemnation appears in **Surat al-Baqarah**, revealed in the later years of the Prophet's life, shortly before his Farewell Sermon. The verses are sweeping and uncompromising:

> *"Those who consume riba will not stand [on the Day of Judgment] except as one who is being beaten by Satan into madness. That is because they say, 'Trade is just like riba,' but Allah has permitted trade and forbidden riba..."* ***(Surah al-Baqarah 2:275)***

The language is stark. Those who deal in *riba* are likened to individuals under satanic possession—disoriented, unstable, spiritually diseased. The verse also acknowledges a popular justification of the time: that interest is no different from profit in trade. The Qur'an dismantles this argument by making a categorical distinction: trade involves risk and effort; *riba* guarantees gain with no liability.

The same passage continues with escalating warnings:

> *"If you do not give up what remains of riba, then be informed of a war from Allah and His Messenger."* ***(Surah al-Baqarah 2:279)***

This verse stands alone in Islamic scripture. No other sin—neither theft, adultery, nor even murder—is described as invoking a declaration of war from God and His Messenger. The language is deliberately forceful. It signifies that *riba* is not merely a financial violation, but a rebellion against the divine moral order.

The Qur'anic opposition to *riba* is not isolated to condemnation; it is part of a broader vision of economic justice. The surrounding verses promote fairness in contracts, encourage voluntary charity (*sadaqah*), and stipulate the proper treatment of debtors. A few verses after the condemnation of *riba*, the Qur'an reveals one of the most detailed legal passages in the entire scripture—**Ayat al-Dayn (2:282)**—which outlines how debts should be recorded, witnessed, and repaid.

The revelation does not leave the question of indebtedness unresolved. In **Surah al-Baqarah 2:280**, it offers this instruction:

> *"And if the debtor is in hardship, then [let there be] postponement until [a time of] ease. But if you remit it by way of charity, it is better for you, if you only knew."*

This verse provides an ethical imperative for lenders: patience with those who are struggling and encouragement toward forgiveness. It challenges the logic of profit-driven lending by placing mercy above gain.

The Prophet Muhammad (pbuh) enforced these verses not only through legal reform but through his personal practice. He forbade the practice of *riba* in his Farewell Sermon, where he declared:

> *"All riba of the Days of Ignorance is abolished. And the first riba I abolish is that of al-'Abbas ibn 'Abd al-Muttalib [his own uncle]."*

This public renunciation was not symbolic; it set a precedent. By cancelling the interest owed to his own family, the Prophet established a model of leadership grounded in principle, not privilege.

The Quranic revelation on *riba* marked a fundamental rupture with pre-Islamic economic norms. It reoriented the basis of commercial ethics from exploitation to equity, from coercion to compassion. It was not merely a financial reform—it was a redefinition of what it meant to deal justly with others in both worldly and spiritual terms.

Chapter 5: The Prophetic Legacy — Hadith on Interest and Economic Justice

The Qur'an laid the foundational prohibitions against *riba*, but the Hadith—the sayings, actions, and approvals of the Prophet Muhammad (pbuh)—served to interpret, implement, and expand these teachings into a lived economic framework. Together, they formed a comprehensive model of justice that penetrated not only religious rituals but everyday financial transactions. While the Qur'an provided the moral compass, the Hadith gave it texture and enforcement through examples and legal elaboration.

Among the earliest and most explicit narrations is the well-known Hadith:

> *"The Messenger of Allah cursed the one who consumes riba, the one who gives it, the one who records it, and the two witnesses to it, and he said: 'They are all the same.'"*
>
> ***(Sahih Muslim, 1598)***

This Hadith expanded the circle of accountability. It refused to isolate guilt to the one profiting from interest. Instead, it drew in the entire ecosystem that enables interest-bearing transactions. The scribe who documents the contract and the witnesses who observe it are placed on equal moral footing with the lender and borrower. In doing so, the Prophet (pbuh) condemned *riba* not just as a harmful act but as a corrupt financial culture that needed total rejection.

Another Hadith emphasizes the scale of the sin:

> *"Riba has seventy-three doors, the least of which is like a man committing incest with his mother."*
>
> ***(Musnad Ahmad, 21957; Al-Tabarani in Al-Awsat)***

This visceral metaphor is not rhetorical excess—it is deliberate moral shock. It indicates the magnitude of *riba* as a social sin that violates not only individual dignity but the sanctity of communal justice. It undermines the fabric of society by institutionalizing exploitation.

The Prophet Muhammad (pbuh) made it a point to distinguish between legitimate trade and exploitative lending. In several narrations, he clarified the difference between profit earned through productive exchange and profit derived from guaranteed returns without effort or risk. One narration in **Sunan Abi Dawood** explains:

> *"Do not sell gold for gold except like for like, and do not sell silver for silver except like for like. Do not increase one over the other; do not sell what is not present for what is present."*

This Hadith is part of a larger corpus of narrations known as the **Hadith of Ribawi Items**, which established early rules for commodity exchange to prevent hidden forms of interest. Six items—gold, silver, wheat, barley, dates, and salt—were cited as categories subject to strict rules in barter. These rules laid the foundation for what would become the *fiqh* (Islamic jurisprudence) of *riba al-fadl* (excessive or unequal exchange), a category distinct from *riba al-nasi'ah* (interest based on delay).

These teachings did more than legislate; they educated. The Prophet (pbuh) used financial regulation as a tool for spiritual training. He encouraged simplicity, discouraged hoarding, and promoted mutual aid. In one narration, he said:

> *"The best of people are those who are most beneficial to others."*
> ***(Al-Mu'jam al-Awsat, 5787)***

In contrast to the exploitative lender who benefits from the weakness of others, the ideal Muslim, in the Prophetic vision, is someone who facilitates ease, not hardship. This principle governed debt forgiveness as well. The Prophet (pbuh) said:

> *"Whoever gives respite to a debtor, or forgives the debt, Allah will shade him on the Day when there is no shade but His."*
>
> ***(Sahih Muslim, 3006)***

Such Hadith reframed the lender-debtor relationship. Instead of being one of domination and obligation, it became one of mercy and trust. Financial relationships, in the Prophetic model, were extensions of one's character. A believer's conduct in trade was a mirror of their taqwa (God-consciousness).

In practice, the Prophet (pbuh) enforced these ideals through community norms. He mediated disputes between creditors and debtors. He praised honesty in trade and condemned deceit. He personally guaranteed the debts of certain companions when they died without repaying them, emphasizing the social responsibility of the community to protect both the creditor's right and the debtor's dignity.

He also instructed that wealth should circulate. In **Sahih al-Bukhari**, it is reported that he said:

> *"Wealth does not decrease from charity."*

This statement reversed the logic of scarcity that often drives interest-based accumulation. In the Islamic worldview shaped by the Prophet (pbuh), prosperity is preserved not by insulating oneself from risk, but by trusting in divine recompense through generosity and fairness.

When Islamic governance was established in Madinah, these principles were incorporated into the public order. Trade was regulated in the markets; price manipulation and deception were outlawed. The

Prophet (pbuh) appointed market inspectors (*muhtasibun*) to ensure ethical compliance. Wealth was redistributed through *zakat*, the mandatory almsgiving that contrasted sharply with *riba*. While *zakat* was a tool of purification and sharing, *riba* was a mechanism of extraction and inequality.

The Prophet's (pbuh) Farewell Sermon stands as a final testament to this economic vision. Standing before more than one hundred thousand companions during his final pilgrimage, he declared:

> *"Verily, every form of riba is abolished. And the first riba I abolish is that of al-'Abbas ibn 'Abd al-Muttalib. It is all abolished."*
>
> ***(Sahih Muslim, 1218)***

This proclamation was unprecedented. It was not just a personal or family gesture; it was a systemic rejection of the old financial order. The Prophet (pbuh) set a precedent that abolished not only future interest-bearing contracts but also erased historical claims—no retroactive interest would be honored. It was an act of financial disarmament intended to dismantle inequality at its root.

The Hadith literature thus forms a vital complement to the Qur'anic condemnation of *riba*. Through language, law, and example, the Prophet (pbuh) provided the tools to replace exploitation with equity, and selfish gain with social responsibility. His legacy established a model of financial ethics that held individuals accountable, lifted the oppressed, and connected commerce with conscience.

Chapter 6: The Final Sermon — A Defining Moment

The Prophet Muhammad's (pbuh) Farewell Sermon, delivered during his last pilgrimage to Makkah in the year 10 AH (632 CE), marked a culmination of 23 years of divine revelation and social transformation. It was a moment steeped in gravity and spiritual clarity, attended by over 100,000 companions who had witnessed the rise of Islam from a persecuted call in Makkah to a fully established way of life in the Arabian Peninsula.

Mount Arafat was the site of this historic address. The Prophet (pbuh) stood before a sea of believers in a unified state of devotion, dressed in two simple pieces of cloth, embodying humility and leadership. The sermon was not just a farewell. It was a declaration of principles that would define the moral architecture of the Muslim community for generations. Among the foundational themes he outlined—sanctity of life, honor of women, rights of laborers, and racial equality—was the decisive stance on *riba*.

In the midst of this final address, the Prophet (pbuh) declared:

> *"Indeed, all practices of the Days of Ignorance are now beneath my feet. The blood-revenges of the pre-Islamic era are annulled, and the first revenge I abolish is that of Rabi'ah ibn al-Harith. All riba of the pre-Islamic period is annulled, and the first riba I annul is that of al-'Abbas ibn 'Abd al-Muttalib."*

This was no minor clause in the speech. It was a profound legal and moral reset. By naming his own uncle al-'Abbas—known to be one of the wealthiest men in Makkah—the Prophet (pbuh) made the ruling intensely personal and politically powerful. This declaration did not merely prohibit future interest-bearing transactions; it voided all existing claims to accrued interest under contracts made during the pre-Islamic period. It was an act of economic amnesty, cleansing society of layered financial grievances and replacing them with a clean slate.

The phrase *"under my feet"* was symbolic. It conveyed complete eradication. No trace of *riba* from the age of ignorance (*Jahiliyyah*) would be carried forward into the Islamic era. With this statement, the Prophet (pbuh) stripped *riba* of legitimacy, status, and social acceptance. It was no longer a private or moral concern—it had become a matter of public policy, enforced by the highest authority.

The sermon's significance also lay in its timing. Delivered at the close of Hajj, it coincided with the most spiritually conscious moment in the lives of many Muslims. The declaration against *riba* thus occurred in a context of heightened piety, ensuring its words would echo not only in legal reforms but in the hearts of believers. The sanctity of time and place gave it unmatched weight.

This moment also set a precedent for future Islamic governance. By abolishing pre-Islamic *riba* without exception or compensation, the Prophet (pbuh) established the principle that social justice took precedence over entrenched financial custom. He did not offer compromise for past contracts or gradual reform. Instead, he instituted a bold and immediate transformation. Debts were to be repaid in principle only—without interest. Lenders were not to pursue compounding claims. No legal loopholes were entertained.

The Prophet's (pbuh) companions understood the seriousness of this declaration. Within weeks, the verses forbidding *riba* in *Surah al-Baqarah*—revealed shortly before this sermon—were being cited in legal decisions. The Farewell Sermon became not only an oration of faith but a legislative foundation. The early caliphs upheld its rulings, and Islamic jurists in later centuries treated it as a primary legal source.

The Prophet (pbuh) had spent over two decades challenging a system that enriched a few at the expense of many. His farewell address distilled his economic philosophy into irreversible law. It transitioned the Muslim world from theory to practice. There would be no place for *riba* in the society he had built. What had once been normalized was now delegitimized—not only in moral terms but in concrete, enforceable terms.

In this way, the Farewell Sermon marked more than a closure of prophethood. It was a decisive moment when moral conviction became public policy, when the struggle against financial exploitation reached its legislative pinnacle.

Chapter 7: The Four Imams and Their Positions

As Islam spread across continents, the teachings of the Prophet (pbuh) and the Qur'an were interpreted and applied to new economic realities. From these interpretations emerged the four major Sunni schools of jurisprudence—Hanafi, Maliki, Shafi'i, and Hanbali—each led by an Imam whose intellectual legacy shaped the financial ethics of Muslim societies for centuries. Their analysis of *riba* was rooted in the prophetic teachings but refined to address diverse commercial scenarios. Despite minor differences in technical reasoning, all four Imams agreed on the prohibition of *riba* in principle, treating it as a major sin and a serious violation of Islamic economic justice.

Abu Hanifa (d. 767 CE)

The Hanafi school, founded by Imam Abu Hanifa in Kufa, Iraq, became the most widespread in the Muslim world. Abu Hanifa's background in commerce made him particularly sensitive to issues of finance and trade. His legal reasoning often leaned toward practicality and societal need, but never at the expense of clear textual prohibitions.

The Hanafi school categorized *riba* into two types: **riba al-nasi'ah**, which is the deferment-based interest mentioned in the Qur'an, and **riba al-fadl**, the excess in barter transactions, addressed through Hadith. Abu Hanifa accepted both as prohibited but focused on strict criteria for their application.

In Hanafi jurisprudence, *riba al-fadl* applies only to **gold, silver, wheat, barley, dates, and salt**—the six commodities mentioned in the Hadith. The rationale was that these items served as either currency or staple foods in the Prophet's time. The prohibition was interpreted narrowly to avoid unnecessary burden on commerce. However, when it came to *riba al-nasi'ah*, the Hanafi school was uncompromising.

Charging interest on loans, even by mutual agreement, was unequivocally forbidden.

In commercial dealings, Abu Hanifa emphasized the importance of mutual consent and absence of exploitation. While allowing contractual innovation, he drew clear boundaries to prevent evasion of *riba* through indirect means such as legal trickery (*hiyal*), which some jurists would later debate.

Malik ibn Anas (d. 795 CE)

Imam Malik, the founder of the Maliki school based in Madinah, inherited a unique proximity to the traditions of the Prophet (pbuh), due to Madinah's preservation of early Islamic practice. His legal methodology gave significant weight to the "ʿ**amal ahl al-Madina**"—the established and continuous practice of the people of Madinah, whom he considered inheritors of the Prophet's (pbuh) practical example.

On *riba*, Malik followed the same broad categorization as other jurists but was stricter in defining the parameters. He extended the logic of the six ribawi items to other goods with similar qualities, such as those that are **measured, weighed, or consumed**, thereby increasing the range of commodities susceptible to *riba al-fadl*. His approach emphasized **substance over form**, ensuring that new business methods did not escape the moral purpose of the prohibition.

He treated *riba al-nasi'ah* as especially destructive, and did not allow for any compensation over time in loans, even if disguised as service charges or late penalties. Malik also recognized that economic transactions had moral dimensions beyond the letter of the law. He cautioned against exploiting legal loopholes and insisted that financial fairness must reflect the ethics of the community, not just legality.

Al-Shafi'i (d. 820 CE)

Imam al-Shafi'i, who traveled between Hijaz, Yemen, Iraq, and Egypt, contributed one of the most systematic frameworks of Islamic legal theory. His methodology, based on **Qur'an, Sunnah, consensus**

(ijma‘), and analogical reasoning (qiyas), helped standardize Islamic jurisprudence and bring clarity to complex issues such as *riba*.

Shafi‘i scholars upheld the prohibition of both *riba al-fadl* and *riba al-nasi'ah* but with a nuanced approach to application. Like Abu Hanifa, al-Shafi‘i confined *riba al-fadl* to the six specific items mentioned in the Hadith. However, he was more willing than the Malikis to accept indirect analogies when similar economic effects were evident.

On *riba al-nasi'ah*, al-Shafi‘i saw no flexibility. He prohibited interest on delayed payments, whether in monetary loans or in commodity exchanges. He also developed rules concerning **Bay‘ al-‘īnah**—a controversial form of sale and repurchase used to simulate a loan—warning that such arrangements could amount to legal ruses.

The Shafi‘i school maintained a strong emphasis on **intention and outcome**, seeking to preserve the ethical aim of the law without suppressing commercial innovation. It allowed credit sales and delayed payments as long as they did not introduce asymmetrical obligations or guaranteed returns divorced from real risk.

Ahmad ibn Hanbal (d. 855 CE)

Imam Ahmad ibn Hanbal, known for his deep reverence for the Hadith, adopted the most textually conservative and cautious approach among the four. His school became the most rigid on matters of *riba*, reflecting a high degree of concern for preserving the prophetic legacy without compromise.

Ahmad ibn Hanbal viewed both forms of *riba* as equally serious. His school extended *riba al-fadl* to a wider variety of goods based on analogy, particularly if they resembled the original six in function or market behavior. He rejected any transaction that could be interpreted as a covert interest-bearing loan, even if formally compliant with technicalities.

In Hanbali jurisprudence, contractual intentions mattered immensely. If a trade arrangement—such as two sales tied together or a conditional loan—was designed to ensure profit without risk, it was treated as *riba* in disguise. Ahmad ibn Hanbal saw economic justice as inseparable from spiritual integrity, and thus approached financial law as a moral safeguard, not just a legal obligation.

His students developed doctrines warning against **tawarruq**, **ʿīnah**, and other structures that facilitated what appeared to be compliant trades while delivering the same effect as interest. The Hanbali school often preferred a high standard of precaution (*ihtiyat*) to avoid falling into grey areas.

Chapter 8: Defining Riba — Types and Interpretations

Understanding *riba* requires moving beyond a simplistic definition of "interest" as understood in modern finance. The classical Islamic tradition, rooted in the Qur'an and Sunnah, delineates *riba* into distinct categories—each with unique characteristics and implications. These distinctions reflect a profound awareness of economic realities and ethical concerns that continue to inform contemporary Islamic finance.

Riba al-Nasi'ah: The Prohibition of Delay-Based Excess

The most widely recognized form of *riba* is **riba al-nasi'ah**, literally translated as "increase due to delay." This form occurs when a lender demands an additional amount over the principal in exchange for postponing repayment. The Qur'an explicitly condemns this practice in multiple verses, such as:

> *"Those who devour riba will not stand except as stands one whom the Devil has driven to madness by (his) touch."*
>
> ***(Qur'an 2:275)***

This prohibition addresses the exploitation inherent in charging guaranteed returns for deferred payment, which creates a system where money itself begets more money without productive risk or effort. *Riba al-nasi'ah* resembles what modern finance terms "interest" on loans or credit.

Historical records indicate that pre-Islamic Arabian societies, much like other ancient cultures, commonly charged interest on loans. This was one of the most pervasive forms of economic exploitation, especially among the poor and vulnerable. Islam's early revelations targeted this injustice directly, forbidding the practice entirely.

From a jurisprudential perspective, *riba al-nasi'ah* is considered a major sin (*kabirah*), and its occurrence invalidates the transaction. No compensation for delay is permitted under any pretext, and mutual agreements to pay interest are void. This strict rule aims to protect the debtor from economic oppression and to promote equitable social relations.

Riba al-Fadl: Unequal Exchange in Commodities

A less immediately obvious, but equally significant, category is **riba al-fadl**, or "excess in exchange." Unlike *riba al-nasi'ah*, which focuses on time-based increase, *riba al-fadl* concerns itself with unfairness in barter transactions involving certain commodities.

The Prophet Muhammad (pbuh) delineated six items subject to *riba al-fadl* in Hadith:

> *"Gold for gold, silver for silver, wheat for wheat, barley for barley, dates for dates, salt for salt—equal for equal, hand to hand; if the types differ, then sell as you wish, but hand to hand."*
>
> ***(Sahih Muslim, 1587)***

This ruling forbids unequal exchange of identical quantities of these staple commodities when the exchange is not immediate. For instance, exchanging one kilo of wheat for two kilos of wheat, or gold for gold in different weights without equal quantity, would constitute *riba al-fadl*. The underlying wisdom is to prevent deception, exploitation, and accumulation through manipulation of essentials.

These six commodities—gold, silver, wheat, barley, dates, and salt—were historically either mediums of exchange or staple foods in the Arabian Peninsula. Their treatment under *riba al-fadl* rules recognizes their unique economic and social importance. The requirement of **hand-to-hand** exchange prohibits deferred barter transactions involving these goods to avoid a risk-free gain at another's expense.

Broader Interpretations and Jurisprudential Extensions

While the classical texts specify these six ribawi commodities, later jurists debated whether the principle of *riba al-fadl* could extend to other goods, particularly those that resemble the original six in their economic function or market characteristics. For example, some jurists included other precious metals or staple foods under the prohibition, depending on locality and custom.

The rationale for these extensions stems from the underlying ethical objective: to prevent unjust enrichment through unequal exchange or guaranteed gain without risk. Jurists thus balanced textual literalism with *maqasid al-shariah*—the higher objectives of Islamic law—namely justice, prevention of harm, and preservation of social harmony.

Distinguishing Riba from Legitimate Profit

A critical dimension in defining *riba* is distinguishing it from legitimate trade and profit. Islam encourages commerce, trade, and entrepreneurship as means of wealth creation and social benefit. Profit earned through risk, effort, and mutual consent is praised in Islamic texts. The Prophet (pbuh) himself was a merchant before prophethood, setting a model for ethical trade.

Riba, in contrast, is a predetermined, guaranteed increase without corresponding risk or effort. It concentrates wealth and exacerbates inequality, whereas fair trade redistributes wealth and fosters cooperation.

This distinction has practical consequences. For example, deferred payments in sales (*bay' al-muajjal*) are permitted if the price is agreed upon and disclosed, even if higher than the cash price, because the buyer assumes the risk of delayed payment. However, charging a fee simply for the extension of time on a loan with a guaranteed repayment plus increment is forbidden.

Modern Challenges in Definition

With evolving financial instruments and complex markets, defining *riba* in contemporary contexts remains challenging. Innovations such as credit cards, mortgages, and bonds blur the lines between permissible trade and prohibited interest.

Islamic scholars have developed jurisprudential tools—such as analogy (*qiyas*), consensus (*ijma'*), and public interest (*maslahah*)—to address these challenges while staying faithful to the original prohibition's spirit. The fundamental principle remains: economic dealings must be free from guaranteed, riskless returns derived solely from money itself.

Summary of Types

Type	Definition	Key Features
Riba al-Nasi'ah	Excess due to delay in repayment	Interest on loans, time-based increase
Riba al-Fadl	Unequal exchange of ribawi commodities	Barter with unequal quantities, deferred

Chapter 9: Riba and Contracts in Islamic Law (Fiqh al-Muamalat)

Islamic jurisprudence (*fiqh*) concerning commercial transactions, known as *fiqh al-muamalat*, intricately regulates economic behavior to promote justice and prevent exploitation. Central to this body of law is the prohibition of *riba*, which has profound implications for contract formation, validation, and enforcement. Understanding how *riba* interfaces with contracts sheds light on the careful balance Islamic law seeks between facilitating commerce and guarding against unfair enrichment.

Foundations of Contractual Validity in Islamic Law

Contracts in Islamic law require *offer* (*ijab*) and *acceptance* (*qabul*), mutual consent, clear subject matter, and lawful purpose. Importantly, contracts must not contravene explicit prohibitions from the Qur'an or Sunnah. Since *riba* is categorically forbidden, any contractual clause involving interest or unjust increase renders the agreement void or voidable depending on the circumstances.

Fiqh al-muamalat divides contracts broadly into sales (*bay'*), leases (*ijarah*), partnerships (*mudarabah, musharakah*), loans (*qard*), and guarantees (*kafalah*), among others. Each contract type carries specific rules regarding permissible profit and risk-sharing, carefully designed to avoid *riba*.

The Impact of Riba on Loan Contracts (*Qard*)

The loan (*qard*) is the most direct context where *riba* arises. Islam permits *qard hasan*—benevolent loans lent without expectation of profit or interest—intended as social welfare tools to assist those in need. The lender expects only the repayment of principal, without any additional sum.

Any agreement stipulating a guaranteed increase over the principal in a loan contract is invalid. This rule protects borrowers from the oppression of compounding debts and preserves social equity. The lender's right is limited strictly to recovering the principal amount lent.

Classical jurists emphasized that stipulations for interest—even if disguised as "fees" or "service charges"—are impermissible when attached to loans. The intention behind such stipulations determines their ruling. If the condition effectively guarantees the lender a return beyond principal, it constitutes *riba.*

Sales Contracts and Avoidance of Riba

Sales (*bay'*) are the cornerstone of Islamic commerce and are generally permissible with agreed-upon profits. However, *fiqh* prohibits *riba* in sales when it involves deferred payments or unequal exchanges of ribawi commodities.

Two key principles govern sales to avoid *riba*:

- **Immediate exchange in cases of ribawi goods:** When exchanging gold for gold or wheat for wheat (among the six ribawi items), the exchange must be hand-to-hand and equal in quantity to prevent *riba al-fadl.*

- **Permissibility of credit sales with fixed price:** Selling goods on credit (*bay' al-muajjal*) is allowed, where the price may be higher than cash price, provided the buyer agrees. This profit is legitimate because the seller assumes credit risk, distinguishing it from *riba.*

Prohibitions of Contractual Trickery (*Hiyal*)

Islamic jurisprudence is wary of contracts that circumvent the *riba* prohibition through artificial means or legal stratagems (*hiyal*). Examples include:

- **Bay' al-'inah**: A sale and repurchase arrangement resembling a loan with interest.

- **Tawarruq**: A complex set of transactions intended to produce cash while avoiding direct interest.

The four Sunni schools debated the permissibility of such contracts. While some tolerated limited use for necessity, many jurists viewed them as undermining the spirit of the law and tantamount to *riba*.

Partnerships and Profit-Loss Sharing as Alternatives

Islamic law encourages risk-sharing partnerships as ethical alternatives to interest-based loans. Contracts like *mudarabah* (profit-sharing) and *musharakah* (joint venture) embody cooperation, where profit and loss are shared according to pre-agreed ratios. These structures eliminate guaranteed returns and promote economic activity rooted in mutual trust and effort. Their development reflects Islam's broader economic philosophy: wealth creation tied to real productivity rather than speculative gain.

The Role of Intention (*Niyyah*) and Equity

Fiqh places significant emphasis on *niyyah*—the intention behind contractual terms. Even if a contract appears legal in form, if the underlying purpose is to generate *riba*, the contract is invalidated. Furthermore, justice (*adl*) and fairness (*ihsan*) are guiding principles. Courts and scholars assess contracts not only on technical compliance but also on their impact on social welfare, protecting weaker parties from exploitation.

Contemporary Applications in Islamic Finance

Modern Islamic finance builds on these traditional rules to design products that comply with the prohibition of *riba*. These include *ijarah* (leasing), *murabaha* (cost-plus financing), and *sukuk* (Islamic bonds), which carefully structure profit-sharing and risk allocation. However, ongoing debates persist on the extent to which modern banking instruments replicate or avoid *riba*. Jurists continue to scrutinize contractual forms to maintain the balance between innovation and adherence to ethical imperatives.

Chapter 10: Maqasid al-Shariah: Why Riba is Prohibited

Islamic law (*Shariah*) is not a collection of arbitrary rules but a holistic system designed to promote human welfare and prevent harm. The higher objectives of *Shariah*, known as **maqasid al-shariah**, provide the framework to understand why certain prohibitions exist, including the prohibition of *riba*. These objectives seek to preserve religion (*din*), life (*nafs*), intellect (*aql*), lineage (*nasl*), and property (*mal*). The ban on *riba* aligns fundamentally with safeguarding justice, equity, and social stability.

Preservation of Social Justice and Economic Equity

At the heart of *maqasid al-shariah* is the commitment to social justice. *Riba* undermines this by facilitating the concentration of wealth in the hands of a few, exacerbating inequality. When loans are extended with guaranteed returns, the lender gains without bearing risk, while the borrower shoulders the burden of potential failure.

This dynamic erodes social cohesion and fosters economic disparities. Islam's prohibition of *riba* disrupts this cycle by preventing the accumulation of unearned wealth that comes at the expense of others' hardship. By doing so, it promotes equitable wealth distribution and social solidarity.

Protection of Human Dignity and Welfare

The burden of *riba* often falls on the most vulnerable: the poor, indebted, and marginalized. Interest-based debt can trap individuals in cycles of poverty and humiliation, stripping them of dignity and agency. Islamic law's ban on *riba* is a safeguard for human dignity, preventing exploitation and ensuring that economic relations uphold respect and fairness. This prohibition serves as a moral bulwark, encouraging compassion and responsibility among community members.

Encouragement of Risk Sharing and Productive Activity

Maqasid emphasize economic activities grounded in real effort, innovation, and shared risk. *Riba* allows lenders to profit without contributing to productive ventures or accepting uncertainty. By outlawing guaranteed interest, Islam incentivizes investments where both profit and loss are shared. This aligns capital with productive uses and fosters entrepreneurial endeavors that benefit society as a whole.

Prevention of Harm and Economic Instability

The *Shariah* principle of **darar** (prevention of harm) extends to economic systems. Interest-based lending can lead to excessive debt burdens, defaults, and financial crises. Historical and contemporary evidence demonstrates how unchecked *riba* practices contribute to systemic economic instability. The prohibition thus acts as a protective measure, ensuring that financial practices do not harm individuals or the broader community.

Upholding Moral and Spiritual Values

Beyond material concerns, *maqasid al-shariah* focus on nurturing a just and ethical society. *Riba* is condemned not only for its economic effects but for its moral corruption. The Qur'an describes those who engage in *riba* as transgressors who defy divine command. Islam teaches that economic dealings must be rooted in honesty, trustworthiness, and concern for the common good.

Promotion of Balanced Economic Development

Islam encourages balanced economic growth that respects human needs and environmental sustainability. Interest-driven economies often prioritize profit maximization at the cost of social and environmental well-being. By forbidding *riba*, *Shariah* guides economic actors toward models that integrate ethical considerations, long-term welfare, and the preservation of resources for future generations.

Chapter 11: Historical Fatwas and Court Judgments

Throughout Islamic history, the prohibition of *riba* has been a central issue in religious rulings (*fatwas*) and judicial decisions. These legal opinions and court judgments reveal how Islamic scholars and authorities have grappled with applying the prohibition across varying contexts and evolving economic realities. They demonstrate the dynamic interplay between textual fidelity, pragmatic governance, and societal needs.

Early Fatwas on Riba in the Abbasid Era

During the Abbasid Caliphate (8th to 13th centuries CE), the Islamic empire experienced significant economic expansion and increased use of monetary instruments. The rise of banking-like institutions and complex trade called for detailed legal guidance.

Prominent jurists issued fatwas clarifying the boundaries of permissible finance. For example, Imam Abu Yusuf, a leading Hanafi scholar and chief judge under Caliph Harun al-Rashid, reinforced the strict prohibition of *riba al-nasi'ah* in his seminal work *Kitab al-Kharaj*. Abu Yusuf condemned any form of interest-bearing loan as unjust, regardless of customary practices.

These early rulings often balanced strict adherence to scripture with practical concerns. Jurists tolerated *qard hasan* loans from public funds to alleviate poverty, emphasizing charity over profit. However, they consistently denounced usurious contracts as exploitative and socially corrosive.

The Role of Muftis and Qadis in Enforcement

Islamic courts (*shariah courts*) historically played a pivotal role in enforcing *riba* prohibitions. Judges (*qadis*) adjudicated disputes involving debt and contract violations, guided by fatwas and fiqh principles.

Qadis had to distinguish between legitimate trade profits and forbidden *riba*, a task complicated by evolving commercial instruments. Cases involving disguised interest through sales contracts (*bay' al-'inah* or *tawarruq*) frequently appeared before courts. Many qadis ruled against such artifices, labeling them violations of the *riba* ban.

Some courts imposed severe penalties on offenders, including cancellation of contracts, restitution, and social censure. This demonstrated the seriousness with which Islamic jurisprudence treated *riba*, viewing it as a violation harmful to both individuals and the community.

Fatwas During the Ottoman Empire

The Ottoman legal system integrated Islamic law with administrative governance. The Ottoman *muftis* (legal scholars) regularly issued fatwas addressing *riba* amidst a complex economy involving state monopolies, tax farming, and credit systems.

For instance, the Ottoman jurist Ebussuud Efendi issued authoritative fatwas that reinforced the classical prohibitions on *riba* while acknowledging the necessity of some credit facilities for state projects. His rulings allowed non-interest-bearing loans for public welfare but condemned usury firmly.

These fatwas influenced Ottoman courts, which occasionally faced cases involving interest disguised as fees or penalties. Judges often invalidated such contracts to uphold the ethical principles underpinning the law.

Colonial Era and Challenges to Riba Prohibition

The advent of European colonial powers in Muslim lands introduced Western financial systems, including interest-based banking, challenging traditional Islamic economic norms.

Colonial courts sometimes conflicted with local *shariah* courts on the legality of interest. In some regions, colonial legal systems permitted interest, undermining Islamic prohibitions. Muslim scholars issued fatwas condemning such practices as violations of Islamic identity and ethics.

However, pragmatism led some jurists to seek adaptive interpretations to mitigate harm, permitting limited forms of profit in modern financial contexts while maintaining the core *riba* prohibition.

Modern Fatwas and the Islamic Banking Movement

The 20th and 21st centuries witnessed a resurgence of Islamic legal scholarship on *riba*, driven by the rise of Islamic finance. Institutions such as Al-Azhar University, Dar al-Ifta in Egypt, and the Islamic Fiqh Academy have issued fatwas codifying strict anti-*riba* positions. These fatwas have shaped the design of Islamic banking products that avoid interest through profit-and-loss sharing, leasing, and trade-based contracts. Courts in countries like Saudi Arabia, Malaysia, and Pakistan regularly adjudicate cases involving *riba*, often invalidating conventional interest-based agreements in favor of Shariah-compliant alternatives.

Diverse Judicial Approaches in Contemporary Muslim Countries

In some jurisdictions, hybrid legal systems incorporate both secular and Islamic law, leading to varied enforcement of *riba* prohibitions. For example, Egypt's *Dar al-Ifta* issues fatwas condemning *riba*, but the country's formal banking system largely remains interest-based, creating legal ambiguity. Similarly, countries like Indonesia and Malaysia have developed Islamic financial courts to resolve disputes based on Shariah principles. These diverse judicial responses underscore ongoing tensions between economic modernization and religious adherence.

Chapter 12: The Caliphates and Financial Integrity

The early Islamic caliphates—spanning the Rashidun, Umayyad, Abbasid, and later dynasties—faced the formidable task of governing rapidly expanding territories with diverse populations and complex economies. Maintaining financial integrity was crucial for political stability, social justice, and the fulfillment of Islamic principles. The prohibition of *riba* was a foundational element in shaping fiscal policies and economic administration throughout these eras.

Rashidun Caliphate: Foundations of Economic Justice

The Rashidun period (632–661 CE), under the leadership of the Prophet's immediate successors, set precedents for upholding the *riba* prohibition in public and private dealings. Caliphs such as Abu Bakr and Umar ibn al-Khattab emphasized equitable distribution of wealth and rigorous enforcement of Islamic economic laws.

During Caliph Umar's rule, measures were taken to regulate market practices, prevent exploitative lending, and protect debtors from usurious practices. The administration encouraged *qard hasan* loans—interest-free loans—to support the poor and promote economic welfare.

Umar's establishment of the *Bait al-Mal* (public treasury) exemplified the institutional commitment to financial justice. The treasury collected zakat (almsgiving) and public revenues, which were then used to fund welfare programs, debts relief, and public services—all managed without reliance on interest-bearing loans.

Umayyad Caliphate: Navigating Expansion and Economic Complexity

The Umayyad dynasty (661–750 CE) governed a vast empire stretching from Spain to Central Asia. The rapid expansion brought new challenges in maintaining financial discipline and adherence to Islamic economic norms.

While some historical accounts indicate increased reliance on tax farming and state monopolies, efforts were also made to curb *riba*. Umayyad rulers appointed *qadis* and *muftis* to oversee market fairness and contract legitimacy, ensuring that usurious transactions were prohibited.

Despite pressures from non-Muslim populations accustomed to interest-based finance, Islamic authorities maintained the doctrinal stance against *riba*. However, economic pragmatism led to a diversity of practices, with some tolerated financial innovations under strict scrutiny.

Abbasid Caliphate: Institutionalization and Legal Codification

The Abbasid era (750–1258 CE) marked the flowering of Islamic civilization, including jurisprudence and economic thought. The caliphate's capital, Baghdad, became a hub of scholarship and trade, necessitating sophisticated financial administration.

Abbasid rulers formalized institutions such as courts and public treasury systems to monitor compliance with Islamic laws, including *riba* prohibition. Leading jurists like Abu Yusuf and Al-Shafi'i contributed to the development of *fiqh* that elaborated on the forms of *riba* and legal consequences.

Public awareness campaigns and sermons emphasized the moral dangers of *riba*, reinforcing its status as a major sin. The caliphate's tax policies aimed to discourage exploitation while funding public goods without resorting to interest-bearing debt.

Fatimid and Later Dynasties: Continued Vigilance

Subsequent Islamic states, including the Fatimid Caliphate in North Africa and Egypt, upheld *riba* prohibitions as part of their economic governance. These regimes integrated Islamic principles into their fiscal policies, promoting charitable loans and fair market transactions. Despite increasing encounters with non-Muslim traders and evolving monetary systems, Muslim rulers maintained the ethical framework that condemned interest. Their courts regularly nullified contracts involving *riba* and protected debtors from exploitation.

Challenges and Adaptations

Across the caliphates, balancing doctrinal purity with practical governance was complex. The need to finance military campaigns, infrastructure, and administration sometimes pressured rulers to explore financial instruments. Nevertheless, the core prohibition of *riba* remained non-negotiable. Innovative solutions such as profit-sharing ventures (*mudarabah*), leasing (*ijarah*), and benevolent lending shaped economic policies, allowing the caliphates to manage public finance without violating Islamic tenets.

Chapter 13: The Rise of Islamic Markets and Credit Systems

The development of Islamic markets and credit systems represents a pivotal chapter in the economic history of the Muslim world. Rooted deeply in the prohibition of *riba*, these systems evolved to facilitate trade and commerce while upholding the ethical standards prescribed by Islamic law. This growth was instrumental in fostering economic dynamism, social cohesion, and financial integrity within Muslim societies.

Emergence of Islamic Markets

Islamic markets (*suqs*) emerged as vibrant centers of trade and exchange throughout the early and medieval Islamic eras. These marketplaces were not merely physical locations but also hubs of legal and ethical oversight.

Merchants operated under a shared code of conduct derived from *Shariah*, emphasizing fairness, honesty, and the avoidance of exploitative practices such as *riba*. Market regulators and religious officials supervised transactions, ensuring compliance with Islamic prohibitions and promoting consumer protection.

The markets' growth was supported by a standardized system of weights and measures, contracts, and dispute resolution mechanisms, creating an environment of trust critical for commerce.

Development of Credit Instruments Without Interest

The prohibition of *riba* necessitated the innovation of credit mechanisms that allowed economic actors to transact on deferred payment terms without incurring interest.

One key instrument was the *salam* contract, a forward sale where payment was made in advance for goods delivered later. This arrangement provided sellers with immediate capital while buyers secured future supply, all without interest.

Another vital contract was *istisna'*, used for manufacturing and construction projects, where buyers commissioned goods or works to be completed at a future date with payment terms agreed upon upfront. Both *salam* and *istisna'* circumvented the need for interest-based loans by embedding finance within commercial contracts.

Role of Partnerships and Profit-Sharing

To meet the demand for investment capital without *riba*, Muslim merchants and financiers developed partnership structures such as *mudarabah* and *musharakah*. These arrangements distributed profits and losses between investors and entrepreneurs, aligning incentives and risks fairly.

Mudarabah allowed an investor to provide capital to an entrepreneur who managed the business, sharing profits according to agreed ratios while the investor bore financial losses. *Musharakah* involved joint ownership and shared management, with all partners participating in profit and loss. Such models promoted entrepreneurial activity and economic diversification, fostering resilience and ethical financial relations.

Credit Networks and Trust-Based Lending

In many Islamic societies, credit was often extended based on personal relationships and community trust rather than formal collateral or interest payments. Extended family, tribal, and guild affiliations formed the backbone of such informal credit networks. Lenders offered *qard hasan* (benevolent loans) to needy individuals, expecting only the principal to be repaid. These loans reinforced social solidarity and helped individuals weather economic hardships without falling into the trap of usurious debt. Religious exhortations and community pressure discouraged default and ensured repayment, maintaining the viability of such credit systems.

Institutional Support and the Role of Waqf

The *waqf* system—endowments established for charitable purposes—played a significant role in supporting economic activity and credit availability. Waqf properties generated revenue used to fund public services, education, and interest-free loans to the poor. These institutions complemented the formal markets by providing a social safety net that mitigated economic risks and reduced reliance on exploitative lending.

Challenges in Expanding Credit Markets

Despite these innovations, Islamic credit systems faced challenges, particularly in large-scale commerce requiring significant capital. The absence of standardized credit scoring, collateral requirements, and enforceable legal frameworks occasionally limited access to credit, especially for distant or less connected traders. Nonetheless, Muslim societies continually adapted, blending religious principles with practical needs to sustain economic growth without compromising on the prohibition of *riba*.

Chapter 14: Colonialism and the Infiltration of Interest-Based Systems

The era of European colonialism brought profound economic and legal transformations to Muslim lands, fundamentally altering indigenous financial systems and challenging Islamic prohibitions on *riba*. As colonial powers expanded their dominion across Asia, Africa, and the Middle East from the 16th century onward, they introduced Western economic models centered on interest-based finance. This infiltration precipitated tensions between traditional Islamic economic ethics and the demands of modern capitalism.

Colonial Economic Policies and Financial Imposition

Colonial administrations sought to integrate Muslim territories into global trade networks to serve imperial interests. This integration required establishing financial institutions modeled on European banking systems, which inherently relied on interest charges as the cost of capital.

Colonial governments often imposed legal frameworks that legitimized interest-bearing loans for public infrastructure, commercial enterprises, and government borrowing. These imposed financial laws clashed directly with Islamic legal prohibitions, marginalizing indigenous practices and undermining traditional credit systems.

Dismantling Indigenous Financial Institutions

Many local Islamic financial structures, including *waqfs*, charitable lending networks, and partnership-based credit, suffered under colonial regimes. The introduction of formal banking systems reduced the role of trust-based and risk-sharing arrangements fundamental to Islamic finance. Colonial authorities frequently confiscated or restructured *waqf* properties to redirect revenues toward colonial coffers. This undermined community welfare mechanisms that previously facilitated interest-free lending and social support.

Legal Pluralism and Jurisdictional Conflicts

Colonial administrations introduced dual legal systems: secular courts operating under colonial law and Islamic courts restricted to personal status issues. In financial matters, colonial courts often superseded Islamic judicial authority, enforcing contracts that involved interest despite religious prohibitions. This jurisdictional fragmentation weakened the enforcement of *riba* bans and created confusion among Muslim populations about the legitimacy of interest-based transactions.

Muslim Responses and Scholarly Resistance

Faced with the erosion of Islamic economic principles, Muslim scholars and reformers articulated vigorous critiques of colonial financial practices. Prominent jurists issued fatwas condemning colonial interest-based loans and calling for the preservation of Islamic financial ethics. Movements to revive Islamic law and resist colonial economic domination often centered on reaffirming the prohibition of *riba*. In parallel, some scholars sought to reinterpret Islamic economic jurisprudence to engage with modern financial realities, aiming to protect Muslim interests without compromising core religious values.

Economic and Social Impacts on Muslim Communities

The infiltration of interest-based systems contributed to widening economic disparities within colonized Muslim societies. Small-scale traders and farmers, unfamiliar with or excluded from colonial banking, often became vulnerable to high-interest loans from informal lenders, perpetuating cycles of debt and poverty. The breakdown of traditional credit networks and community-based welfare intensified social fragmentation and economic dependency, undermining the ethical fabric that Islamic finance aimed to preserve.

Seeds of the Islamic Finance Revival

The colonial period's challenges planted the seeds for the modern Islamic finance movement. In the face of pervasive interest-based economies, Muslim intellectuals began developing alternative financial models aligned with Islamic law. These early efforts laid the groundwork for post-colonial attempts to establish Shariah-compliant banking and credit institutions, aiming to restore financial integrity and social justice within Muslim communities.

Chapter 15: Muslim Resistance and Reformers

In response to the widespread imposition of interest-based financial systems during the colonial period, Muslim intellectuals, jurists, and community leaders spearheaded efforts to resist the encroachment of *riba* and revive Islamic economic principles. This resistance was not merely a rejection of foreign economic models but a broader movement aimed at reclaiming religious identity, social justice, and financial sovereignty.

Early Intellectual Challenges

From the late 19th century onwards, a wave of Muslim scholars began articulating critiques of colonial economic policies, highlighting the inherent injustice of *riba* and its corrosive effects on Muslim societies. Figures such as Jamal al-Din al-Afghani and Muhammad Abduh championed the revival of Islamic law, including its prohibition of interest, as essential for moral and political independence. They argued that economic liberation required returning to the ethical foundations of Islam, including fair financial dealings free from usury.

Reformist Movements and Legal Reassertion

Across regions, reform movements emerged to reassert Islamic economic norms. In Egypt, scholars at Al-Azhar University issued renewed fatwas condemning *riba* and challenging the legitimacy of interest-based banks operating under colonial and post-colonial regimes. Similarly, in the Indian subcontinent, reformist organizations such as the Deobandi and Jamaat-e-Islami sought to educate Muslims about the religious imperatives against *riba*, encouraging adherence to Islamic commercial ethics even under challenging economic conditions. These movements combined religious revivalism with social reform, promoting interest-free lending, cooperative economics, and charitable initiatives as alternatives to colonial financial models.

Grassroots Activism and Community Initiatives

Beyond scholarly circles, community leaders organized grassroots campaigns to resist exploitative lending practices. Informal credit unions, benevolent societies, and mutual aid groups proliferated, providing interest-free loans and financial assistance rooted in Islamic principles. These community-driven efforts strengthened social solidarity and offered practical alternatives to the usurious debt traps exacerbated by colonial economic policies.

Political Advocacy and Institutional Foundations

In the mid-20th century, the rise of Muslim-majority nation-states provided new platforms for challenging interest-based finance. Political leaders and Islamic parties incorporated the prohibition of *riba* into national discourse, advocating for legal reforms. Institutions such as the Islamic Fiqh Academy were established to provide scholarly guidance on financial matters, issuing authoritative fatwas that rejected conventional interest while endorsing Shariah-compliant financial innovation. These bodies laid the intellectual groundwork for the eventual establishment of Islamic banking systems, seeking to institutionalize economic justice on a broad scale.

Reinterpretation and Adaptation

Some reformers pursued reinterpretations of traditional jurisprudence to address modern financial complexities without compromising the core prohibition of *riba*. They explored how profit-and-loss sharing, leasing, and trade-based contracts could serve as viable alternatives, harmonizing Islamic ethics with contemporary economic realities. This adaptive approach enabled the development of an Islamic financial framework capable of engaging with global markets while preserving religious integrity.

Influence on Modern Islamic Finance

The resistance and reform efforts of this era directly contributed to the emergence of the Islamic banking and finance industry in the late 20th century. By reviving and contextualizing the prohibition of *riba*,

Muslim reformers inspired a new generation of scholars, entrepreneurs, and policymakers committed to creating financial systems rooted in Islamic law and social justice.

Chapter 16: The Rise of Central Banks and Fiat Currency

The emergence of central banking and the widespread adoption of fiat currency in the modern era marked a profound transformation in global financial systems. These developments posed unique challenges to Islamic economic principles, particularly the prohibition of *riba*, as they introduced novel forms of credit creation and monetary policy that often relied on interest as a fundamental mechanism.

Origins of Central Banking

The concept of central banking originated in Europe during the 17th century, notably with the establishment of the Bank of England in 1694. Central banks were designed to stabilize national economies by regulating money supply, acting as lenders of last resort, and managing government debt. By the 20th century, central banks had become pivotal institutions controlling monetary policy, issuing currency, and overseeing commercial banks. Their influence extended globally, shaping financial markets and sovereign economies alike.

Fiat Currency and Its Implications

Unlike commodity-backed money such as gold or silver, fiat currency derives its value from government decree rather than intrinsic worth. Central banks issue fiat money, which is not convertible into physical assets but is accepted as legal tender within a jurisdiction. This system enables flexible monetary policy but also introduces the possibility of currency devaluation, inflation, and credit expansion through debt creation. Since central banks often charge interest on money lent to commercial banks or governments, the system inherently involves *riba*-based transactions at its core.

Interest as a Monetary Policy Tool

Central banks employ interest rates to control inflation, stimulate economic growth, or curb excessive borrowing. The setting of benchmark interest rates influences borrowing costs throughout the economy, affecting everything from consumer loans to corporate financing. This reliance on interest rates places *riba* at the heart of contemporary monetary policy, directly conflicting with Islamic prohibitions.

Challenges for Islamic Finance

The rise of central banking and fiat currency posed intricate challenges for Muslim societies striving to maintain Shariah-compliant economic systems. The widespread use of interest-bearing instruments, such as government bonds and interbank loans, made avoiding *riba* complex in an interconnected global economy. Conventional banking practices became entrenched, limiting alternatives based purely on profit-and-loss sharing or trade-based contracts. Moreover, the legal frameworks underpinning fiat currencies and central banks often superseded traditional Islamic jurisprudence, constraining efforts to implement interest-free monetary policies.

Responses within Muslim Communities

Despite these obstacles, Muslim scholars and economists have sought ways to engage with modern monetary systems without compromising religious principles. They have explored mechanisms for issuing Islamic-compliant financial instruments and alternatives to interest-bearing government debt, such as *sukuk* (Islamic bonds) structured on asset-backed and profit-sharing models. Additionally, some have advocated for monetary reforms that emphasize real economic activity over speculative credit expansion, aligning fiat money management with ethical considerations.

The Intersection of Sovereignty and Finance

The dominance of central banks also raises questions of economic sovereignty for Muslim-majority nations. Dependence on interest-based financial markets and foreign capital exposes countries to vulnerabilities, including debt crises and loss of control over domestic monetary policy. Islamic financial reformers argue for greater autonomy through developing robust Shariah-compliant banking and monetary institutions, which can resist the moral and economic pitfalls of interest-based finance.

Chapter 17: The Islamic Economics Movement of the 20th Century

The 20th century witnessed a remarkable revival of Islamic economic thought, fueled by growing awareness of the ethical challenges posed by conventional interest-based finance and the desire to formulate a comprehensive economic system grounded in Islamic principles. This movement sought not only to critique prevailing capitalist and socialist models but to establish an alternative framework where the prohibition of *riba* was central.

Intellectual Foundations and Early Thinkers

The Islamic economics movement emerged as Muslim scholars, jurists, and activists responded to the socio-economic upheavals of colonialism, industrialization, and modernization. Pioneers such as Muhammad Akram Khan and Maulana Abul Ala Maududi were instrumental in articulating the economic dimensions of Islam, emphasizing that *riba* was not merely a financial issue but a moral and social problem undermining justice and equity. Their works underscored the need for an economic order based on risk-sharing, social welfare, and prohibition of exploitative interest.

Integration with Broader Islamic Revival

The movement was closely linked with broader Islamic revivalism, which sought to reclaim Islamic identity and law in the face of Western secularism and colonial legacies. Economic reform was seen as inseparable from political and cultural renewal, with the rejection of *riba* symbolizing resistance against unjust economic domination and a return to authentic Islamic values. Institutions, journals, and conferences emerged to promote these ideas, fostering networks of scholars committed to Islamic economic reform.

Conceptual Developments and Theoretical Models

During this period, Islamic economists developed theoretical models that integrated classical Islamic jurisprudence with modern economic analysis. They elaborated on concepts such as *mudarabah* (profit-sharing), *musharakah* (joint venture), *zakat* (almsgiving), and *waqf* (endowment) as foundational pillars supporting a just economy free from *riba*. Their writings addressed issues of money supply, inflation, distribution of wealth, and social justice, attempting to build a coherent economic philosophy aligned with Shariah.

Institutional and Practical Initiatives

The Islamic economics movement spurred the creation of practical institutions aimed at implementing its ideals. In the mid-20th century, efforts began to establish Islamic banks and financial institutions offering interest-free banking services. Pioneering projects such as the Mit Ghamr Savings Bank in Egypt (established in 1963) demonstrated the viability of interest-free finance and inspired similar initiatives across the Muslim world.

Challenges and Critiques

Despite enthusiasm, the movement faced significant challenges, including skepticism from orthodox scholars, logistical hurdles in competing with conventional banks, and the difficulty of adapting Islamic principles to complex modern financial systems. Critics argued that early Islamic economics lacked empirical rigor or were overly idealistic, while proponents continuously refined their approaches to address practical economic realities.

Legacy and Ongoing Influence

By the close of the 20th century, the Islamic economics movement had laid the intellectual and institutional groundwork for the contemporary Islamic finance industry. It rekindled a discourse on *riba* that connected traditional jurisprudence with modern economic challenges, inspiring generations of scholars, policymakers, and entrepreneurs. This revival reshaped Muslim engagement with global finance, emphasizing ethical imperatives alongside economic development.

Chapter 18: The Creation of Islamic Banking

The creation of Islamic banking represents one of the most significant milestones in the contemporary Muslim world's effort to operationalize the prohibition of *riba* within modern financial systems. Rooted in centuries-old jurisprudential principles, Islamic banking emerged as a practical alternative to conventional interest-based institutions, offering financial services compliant with Shariah law and ethical standards.

Early Experiments and Conceptual Foundations

The foundation for Islamic banking was laid by early 20th-century scholars who advocated for financial models free from interest. However, it was not until the mid-20th century that concrete institutions began to materialize.

The Mit Ghamr Savings Bank in Egypt, established in 1963 by Ahmad Elnaggar, is widely recognized as the first experiment in interest-free banking. The bank operated on principles of profit-and-loss sharing and interest-free loans, attracting modest local deposits and providing finance aligned with Islamic ethical guidelines. This pioneering initiative demonstrated that banking could function without *riba*, sparking interest across the Muslim world.

The Pioneering Institutions

Following Mit Ghamr, other institutions emerged to formalize Islamic banking practices. In 1975, the establishment of Dubai Islamic Bank marked a critical advancement. It was the first commercial bank to operate fully under Shariah principles, offering a range of financial products excluding interest. Shortly thereafter, the Islamic Development Bank was founded in 1977, with a mandate to promote economic development and social progress in Muslim countries through Shariah-compliant finance. These early institutions combined religious legitimacy with practical financial services, building customer trust and institutional credibility.

Key Principles and Contractual Mechanisms

Islamic banking is grounded in several core principles derived from classical Islamic jurisprudence:

- The prohibition of *riba*, meaning no interest can be charged or paid.
- Profit-and-loss sharing, as embodied in *mudarabah* and *musharakah* contracts.
- Asset-backed financing, ensuring that transactions involve tangible economic activity rather than speculation.
- Avoidance of uncertainty (*gharar*) and gambling (*maysir*), promoting transparency and fairness.

Common Islamic banking contracts include:

- *Murabaha*: Cost-plus financing where the bank purchases an asset and sells it to the customer at an agreed markup.
- *Ijara*: Leasing contracts where the bank owns an asset and leases it to the client.
- *Istisna‘* and *salam*: Forward contracts used in manufacturing and agriculture.

These mechanisms enable banks to provide financial services while adhering strictly to Shariah.

Regulatory and Governance Frameworks

To ensure compliance, Islamic banks established Shariah supervisory boards composed of qualified jurists who review products, contracts, and operations. These boards issue fatwas (legal opinions) that certify the Shariah compatibility of banking activities, providing customers and regulators with assurance. Governance structures also emphasize ethical conduct, social responsibility, and equitable treatment of stakeholders.

Expansion and Globalization

From their initial roots in the Middle East and North Africa, Islamic banks expanded rapidly in the 1980s and 1990s, establishing branches and subsidiaries worldwide. Markets in Southeast Asia, Europe, and North America witnessed growing demand for Shariah-compliant products, prompting conventional banks to develop Islamic windows or affiliated subsidiaries. The rise of Islamic banking represented a global movement, reflecting the diversity and adaptability of Islamic finance principles.

Challenges and Adaptations

The creation of Islamic banking was not without challenges. Issues such as standardization of contracts, liquidity management, and integration with global financial markets required continuous innovation. Debates over interpretations of *riba*, the authenticity of certain financial products, and balancing profit with ethical imperatives spurred ongoing scholarship and practical adjustments. Despite obstacles, Islamic banking established itself as a viable, growing sector offering an alternative financial paradigm aligned with religious and social values.

Chapter 19: Difference Between Islamic Finance and Shariah Compliance

The terms "Islamic finance" and "Shariah compliance" are often used interchangeably in discussions about Muslim economic practices, but they represent distinct concepts within the broader framework of Islamic economic ethics. Understanding the nuanced differences between them is crucial for appreciating how the prohibition of *riba* is applied in contemporary financial contexts.

Defining Islamic Finance

Islamic finance refers to the comprehensive system of banking, investment, and financial services that operate according to the ethical and legal principles derived from Islamic law (*Shariah*). This system aims to structure financial activities that avoid prohibited elements such as *riba* (interest), *gharar* (excessive uncertainty), and *maysir* (gambling).

At its core, Islamic finance seeks to promote economic justice, equitable risk-sharing, and social welfare through instruments such as profit-and-loss sharing contracts, asset-backed financing, and charitable obligations like *zakat*. Islamic finance is therefore a proactive, holistic economic framework with defined objectives to transform financial behavior in accordance with Islamic values.

Understanding Shariah Compliance

Shariah compliance, by contrast, is the process through which specific financial products, transactions, or institutions are examined and certified to conform to Islamic legal requirements. It represents an evaluative and regulatory function rather than an economic system itself. Shariah compliance involves detailed scrutiny by scholars and supervisory boards who assess whether financial operations align with prohibitions on *riba*, unlawful earnings, and other ethical guidelines. In practice, many conventional financial institutions offer

Shariah-compliant products within their broader portfolios to cater to Muslim clients without fully adopting Islamic finance as an operational system.

Scope and Application

Islamic finance encompasses an entire economic philosophy and institutional framework designed to replace or coexist with conventional financial systems. It involves designing financial instruments, governance models, and economic policies consistent with Islamic teachings. Shariah compliance applies more narrowly as a certification process ensuring that particular contracts or products adhere to Islamic legal standards. It can be applied selectively within conventional finance, reflecting a degree of accommodation rather than systemic transformation.

Objectives Versus Mechanisms

The objective of Islamic finance is to create a just, ethical economic environment by fundamentally restructuring finance to eliminate prohibited elements like *riba*. Shariah compliance serves as a mechanism to verify and legitimize financial products within or outside Islamic finance, ensuring that specific transactions do not contravene Shariah rules. Thus, while Islamic finance is goal-oriented, Shariah compliance is process-oriented.

Practical Distinctions in the Market

In the global financial marketplace, institutions may advertise Shariah-compliant services without fully committing to Islamic finance principles. Such offerings typically involve screening conventional products to exclude overtly prohibited features but may not embrace profit-and-loss sharing or avoid interest-bearing operations altogether. In contrast, Islamic finance institutions adhere strictly to the system's ethical mandates, developing innovative contracts and governance to uphold *riba*'s prohibition and broader Islamic objectives.

The Role of Scholars and Standardization

Scholars play a critical role in both Islamic finance and Shariah compliance, but their functions differ. In Islamic finance, jurists contribute to theoretical development, economic philosophy, and institutional design. For Shariah compliance, they focus on reviewing and approving specific products and transactions, issuing fatwas to ensure adherence. Standard-setting bodies like the Accounting and Auditing Organization for Islamic Financial Institutions (AAOIFI) work to harmonize compliance criteria, clarifying distinctions and promoting consistency.

Chapter 20: Case Studies: Malaysia, Iran, and Saudi Arabia

The practical implementation of the prohibition of *riba* varies significantly across Muslim-majority countries, shaped by differing legal frameworks, economic priorities, and interpretations of Islamic law. Malaysia, Iran, and Saudi Arabia provide three distinct models illustrating the diverse approaches to integrating Islamic financial principles within national economies.

Malaysia: A Pioneer in Islamic Finance Integration

Malaysia stands out as a global leader in institutionalizing Islamic finance within a modern regulatory environment. Since the 1980s, the Malaysian government has actively promoted Islamic banking alongside conventional finance, creating a dual banking system.

The establishment of Bank Islam Malaysia Berhad in 1983 marked the country's first fully Shariah-compliant bank, followed by the development of Islamic windows within conventional banks. Malaysia's regulatory authorities, such as Bank Negara Malaysia, developed comprehensive frameworks for licensing, supervision, and Shariah governance.

The nation's success lies in blending innovation with rigorous oversight, offering a wide range of Islamic financial products, including *sukuk*, takaful (Islamic insurance), and Islamic mutual funds. Malaysia also hosts robust Shariah advisory councils and the International Islamic Financial Market, making it a hub for Islamic finance expertise. This model illustrates how government support, legal infrastructure, and scholarly engagement can foster the growth of Islamic finance while coexisting with global markets.

Iran: Institutionalizing Interest Prohibition at the National Level

Iran presents a unique case where the prohibition of *riba* is constitutionally mandated, resulting in a wholesale transformation of the banking system.

Following the 1979 Islamic Revolution, Iran abolished conventional interest-based banking and implemented a fully Islamic banking model based on the teachings of Ayatollah Khomeini and subsequent jurists. All banks operate on profit-and-loss sharing and trade-based contracts, rejecting interest in all forms. The Central Bank of Iran supervises this system, ensuring compliance with Islamic jurisprudence.

While this model upholds the prohibition of *riba* rigorously, it has faced challenges such as liquidity management, economic sanctions, and integration with the global financial system.Iran's experience demonstrates the complexities and practical difficulties of fully eliminating interest within a national economy while maintaining financial stability.

Saudi Arabia: Conservative Jurisprudence and Gradual Adoption

As the birthplace of Islam and custodian of its two holiest cities, Saudi Arabia maintains a conservative approach to Islamic finance, closely aligned with traditional Hanbali jurisprudence. Interest is explicitly prohibited, but the kingdom's financial system has historically been dominated by conventional banking, reflecting the influence of global capital markets and oil wealth.

In recent decades, Saudi Arabia has accelerated efforts to develop its Islamic finance sector, establishing regulatory bodies such as the Saudi Arabian Monetary Authority's Islamic finance division and encouraging the growth of Islamic banking subsidiaries. The country also issues sovereign *sukuk* to diversify funding sources. Saudi Arabia's approach balances adherence to strict Islamic legal principles with pragmatic engagement in global finance, reflecting a cautious but steady embrace of Shariah-compliant financial solutions.

Comparative Insights

These three countries illustrate varied strategies in confronting *riba* within modern economies: Malaysia's dual system promotes coexistence and innovation; Iran's model enforces comprehensive prohibition; Saudi Arabia blends conservative jurisprudence with gradual integration. Each case highlights the interplay between religious doctrine, legal frameworks, political will, and economic imperatives in shaping Islamic finance. Together, they demonstrate the diverse paths Muslim societies take to reconcile the religious prohibition of interest with contemporary financial realities.

Chapter 21: Contemporary Fatwas: Consensus and Contention

In the modern era, as Islamic finance has expanded globally, the issuance of fatwas—formal legal opinions by qualified Islamic scholars—has played a pivotal role in interpreting and applying the prohibition of *riba* within increasingly complex financial environments. These rulings have shaped not only theoretical discourse but also the practical development of Islamic banking, investment, and commerce.

The Role of Fatwas in Modern Islamic Finance

Fatwas serve as authoritative guides to ensure financial products and practices align with Shariah principles. In contemporary settings, fatwas are often issued by Shariah supervisory boards within financial institutions or by independent jurists and councils. These rulings help resolve new questions arising from the evolution of financial instruments, technological advances, and globalization, ensuring that innovation remains within religious boundaries.

Areas of Consensus

Across the global Muslim scholarly community, certain core principles have gained widespread agreement. There is unanimous consensus that explicit interest on loans constitutes *riba* and is unequivocally forbidden. Similarly, agreements exist on the impermissibility of speculative transactions, excessive uncertainty (*gharar*), and gambling (*maysir*). The foundational contracts of Islamic finance, such as *mudarabah* and *murabaha*, enjoy broad acceptance when properly structured and implemented. These shared views have facilitated the standardization and growth of Islamic financial markets worldwide.

Points of Divergence and Debate

Despite general consensus, fatwas reveal substantive differences on several contentious issues. One major area of debate is the classification of certain modern financial products—such as derivatives, options, and credit default swaps—where scholars disagree on whether these constitute *riba*, *gharar*, or legitimate risk management tools.

The permissibility of *tawarruq* (monetization through commodity transactions) also divides opinion. Some scholars view it as a necessary pragmatic solution to liquidity needs, while others criticize it as a disguised form of interest. Additionally, the use of benchmark interest rates like LIBOR for pricing Islamic financial products remains controversial, with some jurists accepting it under necessity and others rejecting it entirely. These debates reflect varying interpretive methodologies and contextual considerations within the global Muslim community.

Institutional Fatwa Bodies and Their Influence

Several institutional bodies have emerged to provide authoritative fatwas and harmonize standards. Prominent among these are the Islamic Fiqh Academy (based in Jeddah), the Accounting and Auditing Organization for Islamic Financial Institutions (AAOIFI), and regional Shariah councils. These bodies issue guidelines, model contracts, and fatwas that influence regulators, financial institutions, and investors internationally. However, the lack of a centralized global Islamic authority means fatwas may differ across jurisdictions, reflecting diverse jurisprudential schools and local contexts.

Challenges in Fatwa Implementation

Implementing fatwas consistently poses challenges in practice. Financial institutions may face pressures balancing commercial viability with religious compliance, leading to compromises or creative structuring that sometimes stretches orthodox interpretations. The variation in fatwas across regions can create uncertainty for cross-border Islamic financial transactions. Moreover, the rapid pace of financial innovation often outstrips the capacity of scholars to issue timely and comprehensive rulings.

The Evolving Role of Contemporary Scholars

Modern Islamic jurists increasingly engage interdisciplinary expertise, combining classical jurisprudence with economics, finance, and law. This evolution aims to produce fatwas that are both religiously sound and economically practical, ensuring that the prohibition of *riba* continues to guide ethical financial conduct amid changing circumstances. Scholars also play an educational role, raising awareness among practitioners and the public about the moral imperatives underlying Islamic finance.

Chapter 22: Economic Inequality and Systemic Oppression

The prohibition of *riba* in Islamic teachings extends beyond a mere financial directive; it embodies a profound commitment to social justice and economic equity. The historical and ongoing struggle against *riba* is closely intertwined with confronting economic inequality and systemic oppression that arise from exploitative financial practices.

Roots of Economic Disparity Linked to Interest

Interest-based lending has historically been a mechanism through which wealth accumulates in the hands of a few, often exacerbating disparities between creditors and debtors. The charging of *riba* frequently leads to cycles of debt that disproportionately impact marginalized groups, deepening poverty and limiting upward mobility. This dynamic has perpetuated structural inequalities within societies, entrenching class divides and inhibiting fair access to resources. Islamic prohibitions against *riba* seek to interrupt this cycle by eliminating the exploitative advantage inherent in guaranteed interest returns.

Exploitation and Oppression Embedded in Financial Systems

The systemic nature of oppression through financial mechanisms manifests in multiple ways:

- Debt bondage: Individuals and communities may become trapped in perpetual debt, forced to surrender labor, land, or assets.

- Unequal bargaining power: Conventional finance often benefits lenders at the expense of vulnerable borrowers, reflecting broader social power imbalances.

- Extraction of surplus value: Interest payments transfer wealth without corresponding productive contribution, creating economic distortions.

Islamic economic principles emphasize fairness, mutual benefit, and the circulation of wealth, aiming to dismantle these oppressive structures.

Social Justice as a Pillar of Islamic Economics

The Islamic worldview regards economic justice as inseparable from religious duty. The elimination of *riba* aligns with broader objectives such as wealth redistribution through *zakat*, the establishment of charitable endowments (*waqf*), and the encouragement of ethical commerce. This framework envisions an economy where resources serve the collective good, poverty is alleviated, and dignity is preserved. Addressing inequality is thus not only a socio-economic imperative but a spiritual mandate.

Contemporary Manifestations of Economic Injustice

Modern financial globalization has intensified economic disparities in many Muslim and non-Muslim societies alike. The entrenchment of interest-based finance in global markets has contributed to crises of indebtedness, economic exclusion, and the marginalization of developing nations. Communities reliant on usurious loans face barriers to entrepreneurship and education, perpetuating cycles of deprivation. Islamic critiques of *riba* resonate strongly amid these contemporary challenges, calling for systemic reform.

The Role of Islamic Finance in Mitigating Inequality

Islamic finance offers mechanisms designed to foster equitable development. Through profit-and-loss sharing contracts, risk is distributed more fairly, encouraging responsible investment and reducing speculative excess. Microfinance initiatives rooted in Islamic principles target underserved populations, enabling access to capital without interest burdens. Moreover, mandatory charitable obligations embedded in Islamic law serve as redistributive tools counteracting wealth concentration. However, the effectiveness of these measures depends on genuine adherence to ethical standards and inclusive economic policies.

Critiques and Calls for Deeper Structural Change

While Islamic finance has made strides in offering alternatives to interest-based systems, some critics argue that it has not fully addressed underlying economic inequalities. There are concerns that some Islamic financial institutions replicate conventional banking practices with cosmetic modifications, thereby failing to challenge systemic oppression fundamentally. Scholars and activists call for broader engagement with social justice, advocating for reforms that prioritize the welfare of marginalized communities and resist commodification of essential resources.

Chapter 23: Riba and Spiritual Corruption

The prohibition of *riba* in Islam transcends economic considerations, deeply rooted in the moral and spiritual framework that guides a believer's relationship with wealth and society. The Qur'an and Hadith repeatedly emphasize that *riba* is not merely a financial malpractice but a source of profound spiritual corruption that distorts the soul and undermines ethical integrity.

The Moral Hazard of Interest

At its core, *riba* symbolizes an unjust gain that arises without labor, risk, or productive effort. Engaging in *riba* fosters greed and avarice, encouraging individuals to prioritize material accumulation over spiritual growth and social responsibility. This moral hazard erodes virtues such as generosity, empathy, and fairness—qualities essential to communal harmony and personal righteousness. By exploiting others' vulnerabilities through guaranteed returns, *riba* damages the ethical fabric that Islam seeks to preserve.

Divine Condemnation and Warnings

The Qur'an contains unequivocal condemnations of *riba*, framing it as a transgression against divine law that invites severe consequences. Verses describe *riba* as "devouring wealth unjustly" **(Qur'an 2:275)**, highlighting its parasitic nature. The Prophet Muhammad (pbuh) warned that those who consume *riba* will face stern admonition on the Day of Judgment, underscoring its spiritual dangers. Such divine warnings serve to awaken consciousness about the gravity of engaging in *riba* and its ramifications for the soul.

The Soul's Enslavement to Materialism

Riba encourages attachment to the temporal world, fostering a mindset that values wealth accumulation above spiritual fulfillment and ethical conduct. This enslavement to materialism distracts believers from their ultimate purpose: submission to God and pursuit of eternal success. The constant desire for interest-based profit cultivates restlessness, anxiety, and dissatisfaction, undermining inner peace and contentment. Islam teaches that true wealth lies in spiritual richness and balanced living, which *riba* fundamentally disrupts.

Corruption of Social Relationships

Beyond individual spirituality, *riba* corrupts social bonds by introducing exploitation and mistrust. It transforms economic transactions into relationships marked by inequality and injustice, breeding resentment and social fragmentation. Islamic teachings emphasize brotherhood and mutual care; *riba* violates these principles by placing profit over people, weakening communal solidarity. Spiritual corruption thus manifests collectively, affecting the health of society at large.

Redemption Through Ethical Financial Practices

Islam offers a pathway to spiritual purification through adherence to financial ethics that reject *riba*. Engaging in trade, investment, and charity based on fairness, transparency, and mutual benefit restores moral balance. The discipline required to avoid *riba* cultivates patience, trust in God's provision, and generosity. In this way, economic conduct becomes a form of worship, reinforcing spiritual well-being and societal harmony.

The Role of Awareness and Education

Raising awareness about the spiritual dangers of *riba* is essential for fostering ethical consciousness among Muslims. Educational initiatives emphasizing the interconnectedness of faith and finance empower individuals to make informed, morally sound decisions. This holistic approach nurtures a generation that values righteousness over material gain, resisting the seductive lure of interest.

Chapter 24: Riba in Everyday Life: Hidden and Subtle Forms

While the prohibition of *riba* in Islam is most commonly associated with explicit interest on loans, its manifestations in daily life extend far beyond overt financial transactions. The subtle and often concealed forms of *riba* infiltrate economic behaviors and social interactions, posing complex challenges for Muslims striving to live ethically in modern societies.

Beyond the Conventional Loan: Diverse Expressions of Riba

The classical definition of *riba* encompasses any guaranteed excess or predetermined benefit derived from a loan or debt contract. However, contemporary scholars recognize that *riba* can appear in many less obvious guises, including pricing mechanisms, contractual stipulations, and financial instruments.

For example, excessive late payment penalties disguised as fees, or markup practices that compound debts without transparency, may fall within the scope of *riba* if they produce unjustified gains. Similarly, hidden interest embedded in installment sales or leasing contracts can transform seemingly lawful transactions into prohibited ones.

Consumer Credit and Installment Buying

In many societies, consumer credit systems facilitate purchases through deferred payments with added charges. While these arrangements provide convenience, they often carry implicit interest components, which may violate the prohibition of *riba*. Installment buying agreements that charge fixed surcharges over the principal amount without sharing risk replicate interest-bearing loans under a different label. The normalization of such credit practices poses a challenge to Muslims seeking to avoid *riba* in everyday consumption.

Bank Charges and Fees: The Fine Line

Modern banking institutions often impose various fees for account maintenance, overdrafts, and transaction services. Distinguishing between legitimate service charges and interest-related *riba* can be complex. If fees merely cover administrative costs and are not linked to the use of money over time, they may be permissible. However, when charges are structured to generate guaranteed excess returns, they may constitute a subtle form of *riba*. Consumers and scholars alike must scrutinize these practices carefully to ensure compliance with Islamic principles.

Investment Products and Hidden Interest

Investment vehicles marketed as Shariah-compliant sometimes incorporate indirect interest through benchmark-linked returns or profit guarantees. For instance, structured products that promise minimum returns irrespective of market performance mask *riba* under the guise of profit-sharing. The use of conventional financial indices for pricing Islamic contracts can inadvertently reintroduce interest elements. Awareness of such subtleties is vital for investors seeking to uphold the spirit of the prohibition.

Informal Lending and Social Pressure

In community contexts, lending among family, friends, or informal networks can also involve hidden *riba*. Situations where borrowers are pressured to repay more than the principal under the pretext of gratitude, gifts, or social obligation may constitute unrecognized interest. Such practices can strain relationships and contradict Islamic teachings on benevolence and fairness.

The Challenge of Modern Financial Complexity

The increasing complexity of global financial systems complicates the identification and avoidance of *riba*. Innovative products, layered contracts, and financial engineering often obscure interest components beneath technical structures. Muslims navigating these environments must seek continuous education, consult knowledgeable scholars, and exercise caution. This vigilance helps protect not only individual faith but also communal economic ethics.

Chapter 25: Debt Culture in Muslim Societies

The dynamics of debt in Muslim societies are shaped by a complex interplay of religious teachings, economic realities, and social norms. While Islam strictly prohibits *riba*—the charging of interest on loans—the prevalence of debt in its many forms remains a significant aspect of daily life across the Muslim world, reflecting both challenges and contradictions within contemporary economic practices.

Historical Context of Debt in Islamic Societies

Historically, Muslim communities placed great emphasis on avoiding interest-based debt, promoting financial transactions rooted in fairness, mutual consent, and risk-sharing. Early Islamic economies fostered alternative mechanisms, such as profit-and-loss sharing and charitable lending without interest, to meet financial needs without falling into exploitative borrowing. Despite this ideal, indebtedness has persisted throughout history, often arising from necessities such as trade financing, agricultural investments, or emergency expenses.

Modern Expansion of Debt and Its Causes

In recent decades, the expansion of globalized financial markets and the dominance of conventional banking systems have contributed to a growing culture of debt in Muslim-majority countries. Access to credit, consumer financing, and mortgage lending have become widespread, frequently operating within interest-based frameworks incompatible with Islamic prohibitions.

Additionally, socio-economic factors—such as unemployment, rising living costs, and limited social safety nets—have compelled many individuals and families to rely on debt as a survival strategy.The normalization of borrowing has altered perceptions, with indebtedness increasingly seen as an unavoidable component of modern life.

Social and Psychological Impacts of Debt

Debt's prevalence exerts profound social and psychological effects within Muslim societies. For many, carrying debt induces stress, anxiety, and feelings of shame, particularly when repayments become burdensome. Social pressures to maintain family honor and meet community expectations may lead individuals to incur debt beyond their means, perpetuating cycles of financial hardship. Moreover, indebtedness can strain familial and communal relationships, especially when financial obligations remain unmet or cause discord.

Debt, *Riba*, and Religious Dilemmas

The widespread reliance on interest-based borrowing presents ethical dilemmas for Muslims seeking to adhere to religious injunctions against *riba*. Many find themselves navigating a challenging terrain where avoiding interest entirely is difficult due to limited availability of Shariah-compliant financial products.

This tension has led to varied responses, including cautious engagement with conventional credit, pursuit of Islamic alternatives, or efforts to minimize and repay debts promptly. Religious scholars often emphasize the importance of intention, necessity, and responsible borrowing in addressing these complexities.

Community Responses and Social Solidarity

In some Muslim communities, informal social safety nets and cooperative lending arrangements aim to mitigate the harmful effects of debt. These include interest-free loans, charitable funds, and mutual aid societies that embody Islamic principles of solidarity and compassion. Such initiatives help reduce dependency on exploitative credit and foster communal resilience. However, their scope is often limited by economic constraints and organizational challenges.

The Role of Education and Financial Literacy

Addressing the challenges of debt culture requires not only structural reforms but also education and financial literacy initiatives. Enhancing awareness about the risks of excessive borrowing, the dangers of *riba*, and the availability of ethical financial alternatives empowers individuals to make informed decisions. Educational programs tailored to local contexts can promote responsible borrowing habits and encourage proactive debt management.

Chapter 26: Financial Literacy in Islam

Financial literacy—the knowledge and skills necessary to make informed and effective financial decisions—holds a critical place within the Islamic worldview. Islam's comprehensive guidance on wealth management, spending, saving, and avoidance of *riba* underscores the importance of educating individuals not only in religious tenets but also in practical financial competence.

The Qur'anic Emphasis on Knowledge and Accountability

The Qur'an repeatedly exhorts believers to seek knowledge and act responsibly in all aspects of life, including financial affairs. The concept of *amanah* (trust) positions wealth as a divine trust entrusted to individuals, who will be held accountable for its use.Managing resources wisely, avoiding extravagance, and ensuring just transactions are presented as ethical imperatives, making financial literacy a spiritual obligation. Understanding how money works and how to navigate economic complexities aligns with fulfilling this trust.

The Prophetic Model of Financial Responsibility

The Prophet Muhammad (peace be upon him) exemplified prudent financial management and encouraged his followers to do the same. His teachings emphasize moderation, avoidance of debt, timely repayment, and generosity. He warned against excessive indebtedness and the dangers of *riba*, highlighting the need for sound knowledge to avoid falling into prohibited financial practices. The Prophetic example advocates for balance—neither neglecting economic planning nor becoming overly attached to wealth.

Components of Financial Literacy in Islamic Context

Financial literacy within Islam encompasses several key dimensions:

- **Understanding of Shariah-compliant financial principles:** Knowledge of what constitutes halal (permissible) and haram (forbidden), particularly regarding contracts, investments, and banking.

- **Budgeting and planning:** Skills to manage income and expenses to avoid unnecessary debt and encourage savings.

- **Risk awareness:** Comprehension of the risks involved in various financial dealings, including speculative ventures forbidden under Islamic law.

- **Charitable obligations:** Awareness of *zakat*, *sadaqah*, and other forms of obligatory and voluntary giving as integral parts of wealth management.

- **Debt management:** Strategies to avoid *riba* and responsibly handle any unavoidable borrowing.

Challenges to Financial Literacy in Muslim Communities

Despite Islam's rich guidance, many Muslim populations face obstacles to achieving adequate financial literacy. Lack of formal education, limited access to Islamic financial products, and insufficient public awareness hinder individuals' ability to make informed choices. Furthermore, the complexities of modern finance and the proliferation of non-compliant offerings contribute to confusion and inadvertent engagement with *riba*.

The Role of Institutions and Educational Initiatives

Governments, religious organizations, and financial institutions increasingly recognize the need to promote financial literacy aligned with Islamic values. Programs incorporating religious teachings with practical financial education have been developed, aiming to empower individuals to navigate the economic landscape ethically. Schools, mosques, and community centers serve as critical venues for disseminating knowledge about money management, Islamic finance principles, and avoidance of *riba*.

Empowerment Through Knowledge

Financial literacy enables Muslims to exercise greater control over their economic wellbeing, reduces vulnerability to exploitation, and supports adherence to religious injunctions. By understanding both the spiritual and practical dimensions of finance, believers can make decisions that benefit themselves, their families, and society. Knowledge, therefore, acts as a safeguard against the subtle encroachments of *riba* and a foundation for building just and resilient economic communities.

Chapter 27: Real Estate and Housing Without Riba

Housing is a fundamental human need and a significant aspect of wealth accumulation and economic stability. However, in many parts of the world, acquiring property often involves interest-based mortgages, which pose a direct conflict with Islamic prohibitions on *riba*. Addressing the challenge of securing housing without incurring interest has become a critical issue for Muslims seeking to uphold their faith while meeting essential needs.

The Challenge of Conventional Mortgages

Traditional home financing methods rely heavily on fixed or variable interest rates, making them inherently incompatible with Islamic law. Conventional mortgages involve a lender providing capital to a borrower, who repays the loan with predetermined interest over time. This guaranteed profit for the lender, regardless of market risks, constitutes *riba* and thus violates the Islamic prohibition. For many Muslims, this reality creates a dilemma between the need for shelter and adherence to religious principles.

Islamic Contractual Alternatives for Home Financing

Islamic finance has developed various contractual models designed to facilitate property ownership without interest. These structures aim to align with Shariah principles by emphasizing risk-sharing, asset-backed financing, and ethical profit generation.

Key models include:

- **Murabaha (Cost-Plus Financing):** The financier purchases the property and sells it to the client at a known markup, payable over installments. The markup is agreed upon upfront, avoiding interest by framing the transaction as a sale rather than a loan.

• **Ijara (Lease-to-Own):** The financier buys the property and leases it to the client, who pays rent that may include a portion toward ownership. Over time, the client assumes full ownership upon completion of payments.

• **Musharaka (Partnership):** The financier and client jointly purchase the property, with the client gradually buying out the financier's share. Profits and risks are shared proportionally during the partnership period.

Each method has distinct legal and financial nuances but shares the objective of eliminating *riba* while facilitating homeownership.

Benefits and Limitations of Islamic Housing Finance

These Shariah-compliant models offer important benefits:

• They provide lawful alternatives to interest-based mortgages.

• They promote transparency and fairness by clearly defining profit margins and ownership rights.

• They encourage responsible borrowing and investment tied to real assets.

However, challenges remain:

• Islamic home financing products can sometimes be more expensive overall due to higher administrative costs or markups.

• Limited availability and lack of standardization across financial institutions may restrict access.

- Complex contractual terms require careful scrutiny to ensure genuine compliance.

Community Initiatives and Cooperative Housing

Beyond formal financial institutions, Muslim communities have also explored collective approaches to housing. Cooperative housing schemes, interest-free loans provided by charitable organizations, and community land trusts serve as alternative pathways. These initiatives often prioritize affordability, shared responsibility, and social solidarity, reflecting Islamic values of mutual support. Though often small in scale, such efforts demonstrate grassroots commitment to housing solutions free from *riba*.

Legal and Regulatory Frameworks

The integration of Islamic housing finance within broader legal systems presents both opportunities and challenges. Some countries with significant Muslim populations have enacted legislation supporting Shariah-compliant mortgages, providing regulatory clarity and consumer protection. In contrast, in non-Muslim-majority countries, regulatory hurdles and lack of awareness can impede the development and acceptance of Islamic housing products. Advocacy for inclusive policies and financial innovation remains vital for expanding access.

The Ethical Imperative of Housing Without Exploitation

At its core, the pursuit of riba-free housing aligns with the Islamic ethical commitment to justice and the dignity of all individuals. Ensuring access to shelter without resorting to exploitative interest-based borrowing protects families from debt burdens and fosters economic stability. Real estate ownership, structured within Islamic financial ethics, can serve as a foundation for wealth creation that benefits not only individuals but the wider community.

Chapter 28: Halal Investment and Entrepreneurship

Investment and entrepreneurship are vital drivers of economic growth and personal prosperity. Within the Islamic framework, engaging in these activities requires strict adherence to principles that ensure compliance with Shariah law, particularly the prohibition of *riba* (interest) and involvement in unethical industries. The pursuit of halal investment and entrepreneurship fosters economic development that aligns with spiritual and moral values.

Foundations of Halal Investment

Halal investment is characterized by the selection of ventures that comply with Islamic ethical guidelines. This means avoiding businesses involved in prohibited (*haram*) activities such as alcohol, gambling, pork products, and interest-based financial services. Investors must also ensure that the structures of investment themselves do not generate or depend on *riba*. Equity participation, profit-and-loss sharing, and asset-backed investments are favored as they promote fairness and risk-sharing.

Islamic Contracts Underpinning Halal Investments

Several contractual forms facilitate halal investment, emphasizing partnership and shared responsibility:

- **Mudarabah (Profit-Sharing Partnership):** One party provides capital while the other contributes expertise and management. Profits are shared as agreed, but losses are borne by the capital provider.

- **Musharakah (Joint Venture):** All partners contribute capital and share profits and losses proportionally.

- **Istisna'a (Manufacturing or Construction Contract):** A contract to produce goods or build projects with agreed terms, facilitating investment in production without interest.

These models align investment activities with ethical standards and mutual cooperation.

Entrepreneurship Free from Riba

For entrepreneurs, establishing and growing a business without resorting to interest-based borrowing is a key challenge. Islamic teachings encourage seeking capital through halal means such as equity investment, partnership, or profit-sharing arrangements. Avoiding *riba* strengthens the entrepreneur's ethical standing and fosters trust among partners, customers, and society. Furthermore, Islamic principles promote honest trade, fair pricing, transparency, and social responsibility in business operations.

Screening and Due Diligence

Investors and entrepreneurs must conduct thorough due diligence to ensure compliance with halal criteria. This involves:

- Evaluating the nature of business activities for compliance.
- Reviewing financial statements for exposure to interest income or expenses.
- Assessing management practices to ensure ethical conduct.

Scholars and Shariah advisory boards often assist in this screening process to maintain standards.

Impact on Economic Development and Social Welfare

Halal investment and entrepreneurship contribute to sustainable economic growth by fostering industries that align with societal values.

They promote job creation, innovation, and equitable wealth distribution. Moreover, profits generated through halal means are encouraged to be reinvested and shared through charitable giving (*zakat* and *sadaqah*), enhancing social welfare and reducing inequality.

Challenges and Opportunities

Despite growing awareness, obstacles remain, including limited access to Shariah-compliant financing, lack of standardized certification for halal investments, and market competition with conventional businesses. However, global trends indicate increasing demand for ethical investments, providing opportunities for Muslim entrepreneurs and investors to expand halal markets and contribute positively to the broader economy.

Chapter 29: Zakat vs Interest: A System of Compassion

At the heart of the Islamic economic system lies a profound contrast between two forces: *riba* (interest), which Islam forbids, and *zakat* (obligatory almsgiving), which it mandates. This chapter explores how *zakat* operates as a compassionate, redistributive mechanism that counters the harmful effects of *riba*, fostering social justice, economic balance, and spiritual growth.

The Concept and Purpose of Zakat

Zakat is one of the five pillars of Islam and represents a fixed proportion of accumulated wealth that eligible Muslims must give annually to specified categories of recipients. Far from being a mere charitable act, *zakat* is a structured system designed to purify wealth, assist the needy, and circulate resources within the community. Its purpose transcends financial redistribution—it is a spiritual duty that cultivates empathy, detachment from materialism, and social cohesion.

Contrasting Riba and Zakat

While *riba* centers on guaranteed, unearned gains that often exacerbate inequality and financial hardship, *zakat* embodies voluntary sacrifice and generosity that redistribute wealth to those in need. *Riba* concentrates wealth in the hands of creditors, creating imbalanced power dynamics, whereas *zakat* actively dismantles such concentrations by uplifting vulnerable populations. *Riba* promotes accumulation without risk, often leading to exploitation; *zakat* requires sharing with the poor, fostering risk-sharing and communal responsibility.

Economic Implications of Zakat

The redistribution facilitated by *zakat* mitigates poverty and reduces economic disparities, which are frequently intensified by interest-based systems. By channeling funds to the needy, *zakat* helps stimulate economic activity, increase consumption, and promote social mobility. It acts as a built-in stabilizer within the Islamic economic order, helping prevent the concentration of wealth and excessive indebtedness that *riba* can engender.

Spiritual and Social Dimensions

Zakat encourages mindfulness regarding the transient nature of wealth and the moral obligation to support others. It reinforces the idea that wealth is a trust from God, not a possession for selfish hoarding. This spiritual dimension contrasts sharply with the mindset encouraged by interest-based lending, which often prioritizes individual profit at the expense of communal welfare. Through *zakat*, Muslims cultivate compassion, gratitude, and solidarity, essential values for a harmonious society.

Challenges in Implementation

Despite its potential, effective implementation of *zakat* faces practical challenges. These include accurate wealth assessment, ensuring transparency in distribution, and overcoming societal stigmas that may discourage recipients from seeking aid. Moreover, in some Muslim-majority countries, formal *zakat* institutions struggle with administrative inefficiencies, limiting the full realization of its redistributive role.

Integrating Zakat into Modern Financial Systems

Innovative approaches are emerging to integrate *zakat* more effectively into contemporary economies. These include automated *zakat* calculations linked to financial accounts, investment of *zakat* funds in sustainable projects, and partnerships with Islamic financial institutions. Such strategies aim to maximize *zakat*'s social impact while maintaining compliance with religious principles.

Chapter 30: Building Community Cooperatives and Microfinance

In the quest to develop financial systems free from *riba*, community cooperatives and microfinance institutions have emerged as powerful tools to empower marginalized populations within Muslim societies. These grassroots models emphasize mutual aid, ethical financing, and social solidarity, offering viable alternatives to conventional interest-based lending.

The Philosophy Behind Cooperatives

Community cooperatives operate on principles of shared ownership, democratic decision-making, and equitable distribution of benefits. Rooted in Islamic values of brotherhood (*ukhuwwah*), justice, and mutual support, cooperatives seek to pool resources for the collective good. This model challenges the individualistic and profit-maximizing tendencies of conventional finance, instead promoting collaboration and inclusivity.

Microfinance: A Vehicle for Financial Inclusion

Microfinance institutions (MFIs) provide small-scale financial services—such as loans, savings, and insurance—to those traditionally excluded from mainstream banking, particularly low-income individuals and entrepreneurs. In Muslim contexts, MFIs strive to design products compliant with Shariah, avoiding *riba* by employing profit-sharing contracts, leasing, and interest-free loans. These services enable recipients to start or expand businesses, improve livelihoods, and achieve economic independence without falling into debt traps.

Successful Models and Examples

Countries with significant Muslim populations have pioneered various community-based financial models:

- In Indonesia, *Baitul Mal wa Tamwil* (BMT) institutions combine social welfare functions with financial services, emphasizing cooperative principles and ethical finance.

- Pakistan's Akhuwat Foundation offers interest-free microloans to the poor, funded by donations and community contributions, demonstrating the feasibility of scalable, *riba*-free lending.

- Malaysia's Islamic cooperatives engage members in profit-sharing ventures, balancing financial sustainability with social objectives.

These examples illustrate how local adaptation and community engagement are crucial to success.

Overcoming Challenges

While promising, community cooperatives and microfinance face obstacles:

- Limited capital and regulatory support can constrain growth.

- Ensuring operational transparency and preventing misuse of funds require strong governance structures.

- Balancing financial sustainability with social goals demands continuous innovation and stakeholder commitment.

- Educating communities about Islamic finance principles is essential to build trust and participation.

The Broader Socioeconomic Impact

By fostering financial inclusion, these institutions help reduce poverty, promote entrepreneurship, and build social capital. They also mitigate reliance on exploitative credit sources, aligning economic activity with Islamic ethical norms. Community cooperatives and microfinance contribute to strengthening the social fabric, empowering individuals to take control of their financial destinies within a faith-based framework.

The Path Forward

Scaling up these models involves integrating technology, expanding outreach, and forging partnerships with Islamic banks, regulators, and civil society. Governments and international organizations can support by creating conducive policy environments and providing capacity-building resources. Ultimately, building vibrant, *riba*-free community finance networks represents a practical step toward realizing an equitable and compassionate economic system.

Chapter 31: Policy, Activism, and Islamic Economic Justice

The prohibition of *riba* within Islamic economic doctrine extends beyond personal piety; it encompasses a broader vision of social justice and equitable resource distribution. Achieving this vision in the modern world requires deliberate policy-making, organized activism, and a committed pursuit of economic justice rooted in Islamic principles.

The Role of Policy in Enforcing Riba Prohibition

Effective legal frameworks are essential for curbing the infiltration of interest-based financial practices into Muslim economies. Governments in Muslim-majority countries have, at times, enacted regulations to ban or restrict *riba*-based transactions, promoting the growth of Islamic finance institutions.

Policy measures include establishing Shariah supervisory boards, enforcing disclosure standards, and incentivizing Shariah-compliant financial products. Such legislation serves as a foundation for transforming national economies toward *riba*-free models.

Challenges in Policy Implementation

Despite formal policies, enforcement can be uneven due to competing political interests, economic globalization, and institutional inertia. Conventional financial systems often dominate markets, and international banking norms prioritize interest-based instruments, complicating full adherence to Islamic mandates. Moreover, the lack of standardized definitions and interpretations of *riba* across jurisdictions introduces ambiguity, undermining regulatory consistency.

Activism and Grassroots Mobilization

Activism plays a critical role in raising awareness and pressuring policymakers to align financial systems with Islamic values. Grassroots movements, scholars, and civil society organizations advocate for greater transparency, ethical finance, and social equity. Campaigns highlighting the moral and social harms of *riba* mobilize public opinion and encourage consumers to demand halal financial services. This bottom-up pressure complements top-down policy initiatives.

Economic Justice as a Core Objective

Islamic economic justice encompasses fair wealth distribution, protection of the vulnerable, and prohibition of exploitative practices. Policies targeting poverty alleviation, fair labor conditions, and equitable market access reflect this ethos. Efforts to eradicate *riba* align with broader aims to dismantle systemic economic oppression, fostering environments where ethical commerce thrives and human dignity is preserved.

International Dimensions and Collaboration

Globalization presents both challenges and opportunities for Islamic economic justice. Engagement with international institutions, participation in global financial markets, and cross-border investment necessitate navigating complex regulatory landscapes. Muslim nations and organizations collaborate to standardize Islamic finance practices, promote ethical investment, and resist pressures to compromise on *riba* prohibitions.

The Future of Policy and Activism

Sustainable progress requires continuous dialogue among scholars, policymakers, activists, and practitioners. Innovations in regulatory frameworks, increased financial literacy, and mobilization of civil society remain pivotal. Ultimately, advancing Islamic economic justice through policy and activism embodies the collective commitment to an economic order free from exploitation and grounded in divine guidance.

Chapter 32: A Global Vision: Reimagining a Just Economy

The challenges posed by *riba* transcend local and national boundaries, intertwining with global economic structures that frequently prioritize profit over justice. To confront these challenges effectively, a global vision rooted in Islamic principles offers a transformative blueprint for a just, ethical, and sustainable economy.

The Limitations of Conventional Global Finance

The prevailing global financial system relies heavily on interest-based lending, speculative markets, and debt accumulation. This framework has been criticized for exacerbating inequality, fostering economic instability, and marginalizing vulnerable populations.Repeated financial crises reveal systemic weaknesses tied to speculative bubbles, excessive leverage, and unregulated risk-taking—all phenomena incompatible with Islamic prohibitions on *riba* and unjust economic practices.

Islamic Principles as Foundations for Reform

At the core of Islamic economic thought lies a commitment to equity, transparency, risk-sharing, and social welfare. These principles challenge the dominant paradigm by emphasizing the ethical dimensions of economic activity. By centering financial transactions on real economic activity, asset-backed investments, and mutual cooperation, Islamic economics promotes stability and fairness.

Integrating Ethical Finance into Global Markets

Efforts to integrate Islamic finance into global markets have gained momentum, with Islamic financial institutions expanding their reach beyond Muslim-majority countries. This expansion introduces models of risk-sharing and ethical investment into broader financial ecosystems. Sukuk (Islamic bonds), equity-based funds, and

Shariah-compliant indices exemplify products designed to appeal to both Muslim and non-Muslim investors seeking ethical alternatives.

The Role of Multilateral Institutions and International Cooperation

Global institutions such as the Islamic Development Bank and initiatives within the Organization of Islamic Cooperation foster collaboration on financial standardization, regulatory frameworks, and development projects aligned with Islamic values. Cooperation among nations is essential for harmonizing policies that enable ethical finance to flourish amid diverse legal and economic environments.

Environmental and Social Justice Considerations

A just global economy must also address sustainability and social responsibility. Islamic teachings emphasize stewardship of the Earth (*khalifa*) and care for the disadvantaged. Incorporating environmental ethics and social justice into economic reform reflects a holistic approach, connecting financial practices with broader human and planetary well-being.

Toward a Shared Global Ethic

Reimagining the global economy entails transcending sectarian divides and embracing universal principles of justice, compassion, and human dignity. The Islamic prohibition of *riba* offers a moral critique of exploitative economic behaviors and a call to reconstruct financial systems that serve all humanity equitably. This vision invites dialogue, collaboration, and innovation to build economic structures that prioritize ethical prosperity over mere accumulation.

Chapter 33: The Final Test: Riba in the End Times

Islamic eschatology offers profound insights into the moral and spiritual challenges that will confront humanity in the final era. Among these, the issue of *riba* assumes a pivotal role, symbolizing not only economic injustice but also a broader crisis of ethical decay and societal imbalance.

The Eschatological Context of Riba

The teachings of the Prophet Muhammad (peace be upon him) and classical Islamic scholars warn that in the period preceding the Day of Judgment, society will witness widespread corruption, greed, and the breakdown of moral values. Financial exploitation through *riba* is identified as a sign of this decay. The prevalence of usurious practices is portrayed as a test of faith and integrity, challenging believers to uphold divine commandments in the face of systemic injustice.

Riba as a Sign of Moral Decline

The expansion of *riba* in the end times symbolizes a detachment from spiritual principles and an elevation of material gain above all else. This moral erosion manifests in unchecked consumerism, indebtedness, and the exploitation of the vulnerable. The Qur'an and Hadith stress that such conditions lead to societal fragmentation, loss of trust, and divine displeasure, underscoring the urgency of resisting *riba*.

Trials for the Faithful

Believers are called upon to maintain steadfastness, avoiding engagement in prohibited financial dealings despite increasing social pressure and limited alternatives. This steadfastness is not merely legalistic but rooted in conscious awareness of the spiritual consequences and the broader vision of justice that Islam advocates.

The Role of Community and Leadership

Communities and religious leaders bear responsibility to educate, support, and mobilize collective resistance against *riba*. Providing accessible alternatives, promoting ethical economic behavior, and fostering solidarity become critical during these turbulent times. Leadership grounded in knowledge and moral courage can guide society through the challenges posed by pervasive interest-based systems.

Hope and Divine Justice

Despite the foreboding signs, Islamic teachings affirm the ultimate triumph of justice and righteousness. The eradication of *riba* and restoration of equitable economic relations form part of the divine promise for a renewed social order. Believers are reminded that endurance and adherence to Islamic ethics are rewarded both in this world and the hereafter.

Preparing for the Final Test

The final era's test involving *riba* serves as a call for continuous vigilance, education, and reform. It compels Muslims to engage actively in shaping economic realities, embodying faith through practice, and nurturing hope amidst adversity. This eschatological perspective anchors the prohibition of *riba* not only in legal injunctions but within a grand cosmic narrative of moral struggle and redemption.

www.ingramcontent.com/pod-product-compliance
Lightning Source LLC
LaVergne TN
LVHW090423210926
848480LV00002B/667